The Other
Pandemic
An AIDS Memoir

Also by Lynn Curlee
The Great Nijinsky: God of Dance

The Other
Pandemic
An AIDS Memoir

Lynn Curlee

Charlesbridge
TEEN

Charlesbridge and the author have exercised best efforts in obtaining rights and releases
from the owners and subjects of all included photographs, many of which are courtesy of the
author's personal collection. Please contact development@charlesbridge.com with any queries.
Charlesbridge apologizes for any unintentional omissions and errors and will correct them in
future printings of the book. This work is a memoir and reflects the author's present recollec-
tion of his experiences over several decades.

At the time of publication, all URLs printed in this book were accurate and active. Charlesbridge
and the author are not responsible for the content or accessibility of any website.

Published by Charlesbridge Teen, an imprint of Charlesbridge Publishing
9 Galen Street, Watertown, MA 02472
(617) 926-0329 • www.charlesbridgeteen.com

Library of Congress Cataloging-in-Publication Data
Names: Curlee, Lynn, 1947–author.
Title: The other pandemic: an AIDS memoir / Lynn Curlee.
Description: Watertown, MA: Charlesbridge, [2023] | Includes bibliographical references and
    index. | Audience: Ages 12 and up | Audience: Grades 10–12 | Summary: "With archival
    images and personal photographs, this memoir chronicles the AIDS pandemic from the late
    1970s to the mid 1990s, up until the death of the author's partner."—Provided by publisher.
Identifiers: LCCN 2022023041 (print) | LCCN 2022023042 (ebook) | ISBN 9781623543501
    (hardcover) | ISBN 9781632893208 (ebook)
Subjects: LCSH: Gay men—United States—Biography—Juvenile literature. | AIDS (Disease)—
    United States—Juvenile literature.
Classification: LCC HQ75.8 .C87 2023 (print) | LCC HQ75.8 (ebook) |
    DDC 306.76/62092273 [B]—dc23/eng/20220705
LC record available at https://lccn.loc.gov/2022023041
LC ebook record available at https://lccn.loc.gov/2022023042

Printed in China
(hc) 10 9 8 7 6 5 4 3 2 1

Display type in ITC Benguiat by Ed Benguiat
    and Gilroy Sans by Radomir Tinkov
Text type set in PChaparral Pro by Carol Twombly
    and Proxima Nova by Mark Simonson
Printed by 1010 Printing International Limited in Huizhou,
    Guangdong, China
Production supervision by Jennifer Most Delaney
Designed by Jon Simeon

We speak their names so
 they shall not be forgotten.

John David Martin
August 9, 1948–September 9, 1994
And all the others.

Contents

Important People

Carl Johnson: A Fire Island Pines housemate, he drank himself to death after his AIDS diagnosis.

David McDiarmid: Robert Cromwell's boyfriend a few years after me, who cared for him during his illness. He died of AIDS.

Doug Capasso: My first real boyfriend and my first real heartbreak.

Doug Peix: Grad school friend and NYC roommate. One of my closest friends for more than fifty years.

Ed Krisher: John Martin's first partner. Our second close friend to die of AIDS.

Frank Cioffi and Joe Bonanno: Party friends who became great pals and social mentors. Frank died of AIDS.

Gail Dessimoz and Michael Racz: A straight couple who became lifelong friends. They own a successful ad agency.

George Shechtman: My gallery owner. I owe him my career as a painter.

Hal Wilson: Our great LA friend and travel companion. Hal died of AIDS.

Helen Martin: John Martin's stepmother.

Joe Palmeri: John Martin's best friend in New York. The last close friend who died of AIDS.

John D. Martin: My life partner from 1978 until his death from AIDS in 1994.

Marc Beckerman: Doug Peix's second partner. He died of AIDS.

Metro Crawford: Doug Peix's first partner. He was our first close friend who died of AIDS.

Nick Rock and Enno Poersch: Robert Cromwell's friends. Nick was one of the first people to die of AIDS in the United States.

Richard Gillmore: Our other great LA friend who ended up in Palm Springs.

Robert Cromwell: My second boyfriend. He became one of the best friends of my life and introduced me to John Martin. He died of AIDS.

Roger Blackmon: Robert Cromwell's best friend and roommate. A Fire Island Pines housemate, he died by suicide after his diagnosis of AIDS.

Tim Bennett and Bill Hunter: Friends from Laguna Beach. They often came to NYC for business. Tim became like a brother to me after both Bill and John Martin died of AIDS just a few weeks apart.

Introduction.
The Years of
COVID-19

In mid-July 2020, COVID-19 cases were surging in Georgia. Eugene Hunter; his wife, Angie; and their son, seventeen-year-old Justin, got tested for the virus. They were alarmed when all three results came back positive. Justin explained, "We were a regular family just trying to stay safe during the pandemic. When my mom would go to the store, she would be wearing a mask and she would be wearing gloves." The family was immediately placed under quarantine. Within a few days Justin's mom and dad had symptoms of COVID-19. Soon both were so ill that they had to be admitted to the hospital. Justin had no symptoms and remained in quarantine at home, alone. He never saw his mom and dad again. On July 26, Justin's mother called from the hospital with the devastating news that his father had died. Four days later the doctor called to tell Justin that his mother was dead. It was only a month before he was to begin his senior year in high school. Justin posted on Twitter in memory of his parents, while thanking his community for their support: "Dear mom and dad, thank you for making me the person I am today. You guys will forever be carried in my heart. And from this day on everything I do is for you. I love you mom, I love you dad. Rest in paradise."

***

Beginning early in 2020, the world was faced with the stark reality of the COVID-19 pandemic. The virus was extremely contagious, and transmitted through the air by breathing, coughing, sneezing, and talking, especially if people were close together and not wearing masks. COVID-19 spread like wildfire, unpredictable and dangerous, as though from sparks carried by the wind. Millions of people worldwide were infected. Some, but not all, quickly became sick with symptoms that varied from mild to very severe. Those with the worst cases had to be hospitalized. A small percentage died. But a small percentage of millions of people translated to approximately 385,000 Americans killed by COVID-19 in 2020 alone. This number grew to more than one million US deaths by May 2022, not including those that went unreported.

We went on lockdown, forced to remain at home. It was hard on everyone, but for young people it was particularly difficult. The virus affected every part of life. You had big plans for the future, but the pandemic didn't care about those plans. School closed down and in many places turned into months of remote learning. Team sports were shut down. You couldn't hang out with your friends. Perhaps someone in your family got sick. You may even have known someone who died. The life you lived before was put on hold. No one knew when the pandemic would end or what the new normal would be. Time passed. Forced to remain at home without the familiar routine of daily life, you gradually became a different person without even knowing it. After things started opening back up, different variants of the virus posed new threats. It quickly became clear that the pandemic was here to stay, and our lives would be disrupted indefinitely.

Forty years ago, America faced a different pandemic disease. For a long time no one was aware that this disease even existed, but it had already arrived, and over a period of years during the 1970s, thousands of people became infected beneath the radar of medical science. Then, beginning in 1980, a few gay men in New York, San Francisco, and Los Angeles became gravely ill. They came down with unusual symptoms and then they wasted away and died. There was nothing that doctors could do to save them. At first it was a complete mystery; no one could figure out why this was happening. And because it was happening to men who had sex with men, in a generally homophobic America many people simply did not care. But after a while it could no longer be dismissed as a gay disease because thousands of people were ill, including many who were not gay.

The disease was first called GRID, for Gay-Related Immune Deficiency, but as it spread, the name was changed to something more neutral—Acquired Immunodeficiency Syndrome, or AIDS. After several years of intensive research, medical scientists determined that like COVID-19, this strange new disease was caused by a virus, one that they called Human Immunodeficiency Virus, or HIV.

This virus, which still exists today, doesn't spread as easily as COVID-19. It is transmissible only by sharing body fluids through sex or by intravenous contact with infected blood. It can hide in the body for a long time—an infected person might live for as long as ten years with no symptoms at all. But gradually it destroys the immune system, and then the disease ravages the body and progresses inexorably to a painful and ugly death. In the late 1970s and early '80s, the virus was spreading silently, relentlessly, and undetected, like a flood slowly rising in a dark basement. But there were no medications to combat it. An effective treatment to halt the progress of AIDS was not developed until 1995—fifteen long years after the first people got sick and started dying. Until then, a diagnosis of AIDS was an automatic death sentence. Unlike with COVID-19, no one survived. People at risk of contracting AIDS lived for years in sheer terror. By the turn of the millennium, a regimen of new drugs was saving lives. But by then hundreds of thousands of Americans had been infected by HIV, and more than half of those were dead. Most of them were gay and bisexual men.

I was in New York City during those years. It was one of the epicenters of AIDS, and I lived through it without becoming infected. But like all urban gay men in the United States, I lived in constant fear for my life, and I knew many people who died—acquaintances, dear friends, and my own life partner. This is my personal account of that terrible time.

To really understand the impact of AIDS, you first must understand how it was to grow up and live as a gay man in the United States in the years just before disaster struck.

It was a completely different world.

1. Growing Up Gay in America

Imagine that it is 1960, and you are twelve years old. Imagine life without social media. There is no Instagram or TikTok. Imagine life without smartphones or texting. Imagine what it's like to grow up with one telephone for your entire family, and it sits on a side table in your living room, with no privacy for your personal calls. How about no computers at all? There is no gaming or any of the other fun or useful things you can do on a laptop or tablet. Television has only three channels, most people still have black-and-white TV sets, and there are no remotes. You can listen to recorded music only on tinny-sounding radios or by playing vinyl discs on a turntable. There is no "online." If you want to find information about something, you consult an encyclopedia, or go to the library.

What if you are a young person who is questioning their sexuality or gender identification? There really is no useful information to be found. Only the certain knowledge that society considers people who are different from the heterosexual norm to be deviants, or even worse, degenerates. Homosexuality is vilified or ridiculed by a majority of people, and the "radical" idea that someone may be transgender or gender fluid or nonbinary barely even exists.

Me at ages 6, 11, 21, and 22 (left to right, top to bottom).

If you are a young gay person in mid-twentieth-century America, you are on your own. There is no sense yet of a community of LGBTQ+ people with common interests and concerns. You find your way by trial and error with really no guidance except your own instincts to determine what it means to be gay. Then, gradually, as you come of age, you figure it out.

First of all, gay is not a lifestyle or a choice. How ignorant! Does a person choose to be straight?

Your sexual orientation or gender expression is not your sole identity. You are a human being first and foremost. But being gay *is* a fundamental part of *who* you are, deep inside. Ask any gay person. We will tell you. We should know. We are the experts.

✳ ✳ ✳

I was a twelve-year-old boy in 1960. Growing up in High Point, North Carolina, we heard about "queers" and "fags," but we didn't quite know what the words meant. They sounded and felt like a dirty joke. Sex was discussed with kids much less than it is today. It was all a big secret that only grown-ups knew. Homosexuality? What was that? So-called sissies were ridiculed and bullied (unfortunately, many effeminate boys still are). We whispered what little we had heard about sex with our buddies. Maybe some of us fumbled around with close friends or in Boy Scouts or at summer camp. There was no Google, and we dared not ask our parents or any other adult what the words we heard meant. My parents never uttered the word *sex* in my presence. Our Sex Ed class in eighth grade, for boys at least, was a perfunctory lecture by an embarrassed gym teacher, illustrated by charts with clinical diagrams of genitals.

For most of us boys, that awkward day in eighth grade gave us the first accurate information we had about sex. Homosexuality was never mentioned by anyone, except as a joke or a slur. For unmarried heterosexual teenagers, pregnancy was a scandal and unspeakably shameful. If a girl got pregnant, she might be sent away to have her baby under the cover of visiting relatives. Some movies had adult themes, but even then there were no sex scenes or nudity, and somewhat chaste kisses were the limit of what you'd see. TV was squeaky clean, and there were absolutely no realistic gay people either in movies or on TV. There was Liberace—the famous campy, effeminate, and flamboyant pianist who appeared on TV, with his opulent capes and candelabra. Was *that* what gay meant? I had thought it usually just meant that someone was happy.

I wasn't particularly athletic, but I wasn't a sissy either. I was a smart kid, I liked school, I loved music, and I took piano lessons. In retrospect I now realize that I had a first crush on our church youth choir director, Mr. Cole.

Puberty arrived with the 1960s, and soon we were teenagers in high school. President Kennedy was assassinated in 1963. I was in Miss Welch's eleventh grade advanced algebra class when the news was announced. Today, when mass shootings are commonplace, it is difficult to convey how utterly shocking it was that such a thing could happen in America. I graduated from high school in 1965 and left home to attend the College of William and Mary in Williamsburg, Virginia. I was there for two years, and then I transferred to the University of North Carolina at Chapel Hill. I had decided to major in art history, and Carolina had a first-rate program, while W&M did not. It was also considerably less expensive, which made my dad very happy.

In the '60s we all listened to the same music. Rock and roll. the Beatles and the Rolling Stones. Motown. Aretha Franklin. Bob Dylan sang, "The times, they are a-changin'." People were questioning the status quo. Young men grew long hair. The new youth counterculture was big news. Hippies were cool, or at least they seemed cool to us, with their tie-dye shirts, bell bottom pants, and slogans of peaceful flower power.

The South was still nearly totally segregated then. Now it seems hard to believe, but I never actually met a single Black person until I was an adult! But as the times changed, it was courageous African Americans who first led the way by demanding their civil rights. In 1960 "the pill" had put birth control in the hands of women themselves. The Women's Liberation Movement soon followed, along with the Sexual Revolution, which questioned traditional standards of sexual morality. Boys got drafted into military service then—you were forced by the government to become a soldier whether you wanted to or not—but the controversial Vietnam War increasingly was perceived by more and more Americans to be a pointless and immoral lost cause. So people took to the streets to protest the war. Our parents frowned and shook their heads.

In the late 1960s the culture was more open about personal freedoms than before. We experimented with drugs. We experimented with sex. I had dated some in high school, but I first had a serious, steady girlfriend while I was in Williamsburg, and then another straight romance at Chapel Hill. Both were lovely young women. Both became dear friends to me, and I am still in touch with them today. But over time I felt there was something "off" in those relationships. I began to accept the gradual realization that I am gay, and always had been, deep inside. During my last two years of college, I first met other young men who were questioning and exploring their sexuality. I remember Andy and Ben and James. We found one another, the way that gay people have so often found one another, then and maybe even now: furtively, secretly, in the shadows. But who wants to live in the shadows?

At this moment in history, in the late 1960s, young gay people became part of the general cultural revolution that was shaking things up in America. There had been small, politically active homophile organizations of gay men and lesbians before, during the 1950s and early '60s, working for acceptance by society, but now an entire generation of young gay people began to assert themselves. Civil Rights, Black Power, Women's Lib, and the idea of Gay Liberation were all related. It was about equality. More than fifty years later these struggles continue.

In 1968 a new play opened in New York. *The Boys in the Band,* by Mart Crowley, was the dramatic account of a birthday party that turns ugly when a group of gay friends drink too much and are brutally honest with one another. It has been criticized over the decades for dealing in stereotypes, and today it seems dated and almost quaint because attitudes about homosexuality have changed so much. But in 1968, *The Boys in the Band* was one of the first ever pieces of popular entertainment specifically about gay people. In the 1950s and early 1960s, artists such as Robert Anderson, who wrote a Broadway play called *Tea and Sympathy* that was adapted into a movie, and James Baldwin, author of the novel *Giovanni's Room,* dealt sensitively with "the love that dare not speak its name," to quote a Victorian euphemism for homosexuality. But in *The Boys in the Band, every* character is gay. (OK, one is bisexual, but confused.) Audiences were given a voyeuristic, in-your-face glimpse of the characters' sad gay lives, a tiresome cliché that, thankfully, was on the verge of becoming obsolete. The play was not uplifting, but it *was* a major landmark. In 1970 the movie version was released, and *The Boys in the Band* played in movie theaters all over the United States. Bob Dylan was right: the times certainly were a-changin'.

In the early hours of Saturday, June 28, 1969, the Stonewall, a small gay bar in New York City, was raided by police. Harsh laws prohibiting homosexual activities of any kind were on the books then. The police routinely entrapped men in homosexual situations and arrested them as a matter of departmental policy. Bar raids, which served no purpose except to harass gay people, were quite common. The names of people rounded up in these raids were sometimes printed in newspapers—public exposure was the most humiliating punishment possible in a homophobic society. Simply being gay could land you in jail or cause you to lose your job, or even be cast out by your family. People's lives were ruined. This time, though, the people in the bar—young gay men, a few lesbians, and some drag queens—fought back. The New York Police Department riot control force was called in to beat people up and arrest them. Over the next six nights, ever larger crowds of angry people assembled in front of the bar to protest and demand equality. The Stonewall riots became a media event, a watershed celebrated today as marking the beginning of Gay Liberation, Gay Rights, and Gay Pride—the idea that one's sexuality or gender expression is not something shameful and immoral, but rather a natural and normal way of being for gay people. Today the Stonewall is an official national monument and a tourist destination.

✳✳✳

In 1969 I got my degree from UNC, but I did not go to my graduation ceremony. (A few thousand of us sitting together in the hot sun in robes and silly hats in a football stadium for some boring speeches? No thanks.) Instead, I took a Greyhound bus alone to New York City. It was my first trip out of the South. I went to visit my friend James, who had moved from Chapel Hill to New York the year before to be an actor. I still vividly remember my first view of

Manhattan, merely a silhouette through a gray mist from across the Hudson River. We went to a big Broadway musical, *Promises, Promises*, and James took me to some gay bars for the first time. There was nothing remotely like that in sleepy little Chapel Hill. I could hardly believe all of those great-looking guys in one place! I was dazzled by New York. It was the end of May 1969, exactly one month before the Stonewall riots.

Late that August I moved from North Carolina to Philadelphia. I had been awarded a graduate fellowship to study art history at the University of Pennsylvania. It was the height of the Vietnam War, and more and more young men were being drafted. As an undergraduate I had a student deferment from the draft. But now that I was in grad school, my deferment was over. This was the moment when the United States instituted a new system to fill the ranks. The US government held a random lottery on December 1, 1969, to determine who would be drafted and in what order. A young man's

Police raid the Stonewall Inn, a gay bar in New York City, June 28, 1969.

fate depended upon his birthday. Each day of the year was given a number from 1 to 365. Every guy I knew was sweating it out. My birthday, October 9, drew number 342. I would not be drafted. If my birthdate had drawn a low number, I would have been faced with an agonizing decision.

Homosexuality offered an automatic deferment from the draft. Today it seems shocking, but being gay was actually considered a form of mental illness, and the bottom line was that the government wanted no "fags" in the armed forces. Because of the stigma of exposure, for most gay young men at that time, declaring their sexuality to their hometown draft board was almost unthinkable. But going to fight in a controversial, pointless, and unwinnable war was also unthinkable. I like to believe that I would have had the courage to announce my sexuality, but I honestly do not know what I would have done if I had drawn a low number. By sheer chance I had quite literally dodged a bullet. Thousands of young men of my generation were not so lucky. 58,220 Americans were killed and 153,303 wounded out of 3.4 million who served in Vietnam.

During my two years in Philadelphia, I worked hard at my studies, and I began to sample big city gay life. Occasionally I went to a gay bar called the Allegro. Gradually I made a few gay friends. I was invited to some gay parties. Sometimes I hooked up with cute guys. I was discovering the fact that many gay men are smart, interesting, and talented, and that being gay can be lots of fun. I was becoming comfortable with my sexuality. In retrospect, I do not recall any anxiety about it. I never had a big moment of coming out, either personally, or to friends and family. It all just happened naturally. I had been raised in a religious family, but I had also been raised to be true to myself. I knew that I was basically a good, decent, ethical, honest person. So I preferred sex with other men. Big deal. So what? I knew for sure in my heart that I was not immoral. The very idea was absurd to me. I came to the absolutely certain conviction that morality isn't really about sex. It simply has to do with how you treat other people. "Do unto others as you would have them do unto you." That was the basic, most crucial lesson of my religious upbringing. My parents had taught me well.

In Philadelphia I made one of the most important and lasting friendships of my life. Doug Peix (pronounced *pikes*) was studying urban design. He had graduated from Cornell University with a degree in architecture and was a couple of years older than me. He was smart, creative, and worldly, but still a bit nerdy, and very funny. We quickly became friends and hung out together all the time. I discovered later in life that my grad-school classmates thought we were boyfriends. But no, while we were both gay, we never had sex. We just clicked as buddies. We were interested in many of the same things. We had the same sense of humor. More than fifty years later, he still makes me laugh like no one else can and remains one of my best friends today.

During the summer of 1971, Doug finished his master's degree. I completed my coursework and wrote my master's thesis on an obscure Victorian-era architect in Philadelphia, a relatively boring subject urged upon me by my mentor professor. I was on track to earn a doctorate in art history, and I still had another year as a teaching assistant to fulfill my fellowship obligations. I was, however, becoming more and more fascinated by the idea of actually making paintings myself. Doug encouraged me. He was offered a job in New York at one of the world's most prestigious architectural firms. I committed myself to becoming an artist. We decided to move to New York together and share an apartment—a small, affordable, two-bedroom place in the Manhattan neighborhood of Little Italy. My half of the rent came to $112.50 a month. I arranged my teaching schedule so that I could commute back to Philadelphia for two days each week and earn my fellowship stipend of $300 a month, my only source of income during my grad-school years. We arrived from Philadelphia in a small truck with all our stuff on Sunday, September 19, 1971, three weeks before my twenty-fourth birthday. We thought it would be quiet, an easy time to move in. Little did we know that the incredibly popular Italian Feast of San Gennaro would be in full swing. The streets were packed, and a brass band was playing right outside the door of our building as we pulled up in front. Welcome to the Big Apple!

Working on my first big painting, Chrysler, *New York City, December 1971.*

2.

"The Only Boy in

Living New York"

From the beginning, I loved New York. I loved the very *idea* of being a New Yorker. I lived in one of the world's greatest cities, and for thirty cents—the price of a subway token in those days—I could get anywhere fast and explore it all. Uptown, Downtown, East Side, West Side—I felt that all of Manhattan belonged to me. The city was broke then. It was dirty and gritty, and certain areas were quite dangerous. Garbage pickup could be undependable, there were many people living on the street, and Times Square felt run-down and seedy. Porn and sex shops were tucked into little storefronts among big X-rated movie houses and Broadway theaters. Our tenement apartment downtown was right around the corner from the Bowery, where homeless people slept in squalid flophouses. None of that mattered to me. I immediately felt at home. New York made me feel *alive*.

Doug Peix and me, Greenwich Village, New York City, 1972.

It was autumn 1971. Doug went to his job in midtown every day in a jacket and tie. I, on the other hand, had plenty of time on my hands, besides my weekly trips to Philadelphia. So I took a couple of months to explore my wonderful new city. I began taking advantage of the cultural riches of New York, exploring in depth the great museums and attending a few concerts and the theater—at least, as much as I could afford. Now it is incredibly expensive, but in those days a young person could move to New York and live in Manhattan with very little money.

It was easy to meet people in New York, and I started making friends. One of the first was Ross. He was a native New Yorker in his early thirties. He worked in a big advertising agency, and I thought he was terribly sophisticated. He and I smoked some weed and went to the Macy's Thanksgiving Day Parade. We got there early and parked ourselves right in front of the main entrance with a front-row seat for the big show. It was hilarious when a gigantic Bullwinkle J. Moose balloon came around the corner, floating high in the air (Bullwinkle was a popular TV cartoon character). One memorable evening Ross and I dressed up in jackets and ties, bought a bottle of champagne, and went to the West Side docks. In those days, before the tragic events of September 11, 2001, caused a mainstream cultural shift around terrorism and travel, anyone dressed presentably could go on a ship before it sailed. We boarded the *Queen Elizabeth 2*, one of the most glamorous of all ocean liners, and walked around sipping tepid champagne, pretending to be rich, before the "all ashore that's going ashore" message sounded. It was absolutely grand.

But it wasn't all play. I am at heart a serious person, and after a few months getting settled and exploring, I concentrated on my painting as winter set in. I had experimented in Philadelphia in my spare time, but now I began painting in earnest. I was ambitious from the beginning. My first painting in New York was a big canvas of the Chrysler Building—everyone's favorite skyscraper because of its jazzy art deco design. However, I was much more interested in making figure paintings, and so I began a series of life-sized canvases, each with a single figure. I was very methodical and planned more and more complex compositions as my skills improved. As I painted, I could see my progress, and I became confident in my technique. During the first eight months in New York, I was still living only on my graduate fellowship stipend. In addition to my weekly days of teaching in Philadelphia, I was supposed to be writing a dissertation, but I never even started it. Now I was a painter.

✱ ✱ ✱

The reality of life in a big city was brought home in a startling way that first winter when our apartment was burglarized. One beautiful crisp day during the Christmas season, Doug and I went ice- skating at Rockefeller Center, in the heart of midtown Manhattan. Growing up in the South, I had never skated on ice, but years before when I was a kid, my cousins and I often went to a local roller-skating rink. I was a bit shaky at first on the blades, but gradually I sort of got the hang of it, and we had a great time. But we returned home downtown only to discover our door wide open, and the apartment ransacked. The thieves had entered from the fire escape in the back by breaking a window facing the flophouse behind us and had exited simply by unlocking the two front-door dead bolts. Nothing of real value was stolen. There wasn't much that was worth stealing anyway—only my college class ring, which I had long since stopped wearing, an inexpensive watch, and a small amount of cash. But the sick feeling of vulnerability and violation was very real. Doug and I immediately took action. We had a third lock installed that was key-operated from the inside, and we spent a weekend constructing heavy wooden shutters on the apartment windows that could be closed and barred whenever no one was home.

When my year of teaching and the fellowship money ended, I needed a job. James, my actor friend from Chapel Hill, knew of an opportunity at Hannett Morrow Fischer, Inc., a small, very deluxe fabric and wallpaper company. I applied and was hired. Beginning in June 1972, I worked in the showroom on East 57th Street cutting samples and taking orders. The business was patronized regularly by the crème de la crème of New York interior designers, but I really was pretty clueless. It wasn't until later that I realized that I had been interacting daily with some famous, high-powered people. My three bosses were gay, and two of them, Mr. Hannett and Mr. Morrow, were a couple. They both were in their midforties and had been together for many years. It was the first long-term, committed gay relationship I had ever known—they were exactly like a married couple. Tom Morrow had a side gig. He was also an artist and designed posters for many hit Broadway shows, such as *Cabaret* and *Fiddler on the Roof*. When I was bold enough to show him my paintings, he was very generous with encouragement and advice. Although I had a nine-to-five job, I kept working hard at my art in my free time.

I was also learning to navigate the downtown gay scene. The neighborhood of Greenwich Village was the center of the action for young gay people then, and I lived within walking distance. On Saturday nights, and occasionally during the week, I found myself at one of many gay bars, socializing, making friends, and sometimes hooking up. Things had changed after Stonewall. The early 1970s was the era when Gay Pride marches were first organized, and many more men and women were becoming politically active in support of the cause of Gay Liberation. The grassroots movement was having some results. The police were no longer routinely raiding bars and harassing homosexuals just for being gay. In the bohemian Village at least, gay people now were living their lives more openly. At one extreme were the flamboyant drag queens, and at the other were the macho leather men, with their black vests, chaps, and motorcycle caps. The vast majority of us were simply guys who happened to be gay. Our standard costume was plaid flannel shirts, jeans (only Levi's 501s with a button fly were acceptable), and engineer boots. Longish hair, mustaches, and the occasional beard were in style. We looked like a bunch of lumberjacks when we went out at night. One day I felt adventurous and got a crew cut. *No one* had crew cuts then, but I didn't really like my hair and was tired of messing with it, so cutting it was liberating. It looked so unusual in the era of long hair that I got a lot of attention when I went out at night, and I found that I really didn't mind that at all.

Early in 1973 Doug introduced me to a young art gallery owner. George Shechtman was renovating his gallery space and hired Doug to design it. He was looking for new artists. I showed him my work, and he offered me a one-man show in the autumn if I could guarantee sixteen large paintings for exhibition. I already had about six or seven that he liked, and so I took the leap and accepted his offer. I quit my job and collected meager unemployment benefits to paint full-time. For a few months I was literally a poor starving artist, and I worked furiously, turning out painting after painting.

In October 1973 I had my first solo exhibition at Christopher Gallery on Madison Avenue. We sold quite a few paintings, which was good for my ego as well as my bank account, and George booked me for another show in 1974. This time I painted a series of life-sized ballet dancers and got a tiny but very encouraging notice in the *New York Times*. The show was a real success. By now George and I had become good friends. We booked another show for 1975, then yet another after that. Eventually I received a commission to paint an album cover for a famous band called Blue Öyster Cult. I was a gallery painter, not a commercial artist, but there was *no way* I was going to turn down the opportunity to paint an album cover for a major rock band. Then a couple of years later I did another album cover for Black Sabbath, an even bigger band. I had fulfilled my ambition. I was a professional artist, I was selling my work, and from then on that's how I made my living.

✻ ✻ ✻

New York is full of incredibly interesting, talented people. After growing up in a small southern city in a time when conformity was the norm even more than it is today, it was fascinating to make friendships with people who were so different from one another, and who had such different life experiences. Most people you meet pass through your life, some briefly, some for a while. Others become longtime acquaintances, and a very few become true friends. I made many long-lasting friendships during these early years in New York. Doug introduced me to Gail Dessimoz and Michael Racz, a straight couple who had a fledgling advertising agency that eventually became wildly successful. They were both native New Yorkers. Gail's dad was a jazz musician. She had grown up in a tenement in the Hell's Kitchen neighborhood of midtown Manhattan. Michael's parents were both from Eastern Europe, and met in the United States during the dark days of World War II. Gail and Michael are still among my very closest friends. There was Gary Miller, whom I had known when he was an undergraduate at Penn. He went to law school in New York, and became my attorney and one of my best lifelong friends. I made friends with Wallace, who worked in the TV industry; Jeffrey, who became a famous,

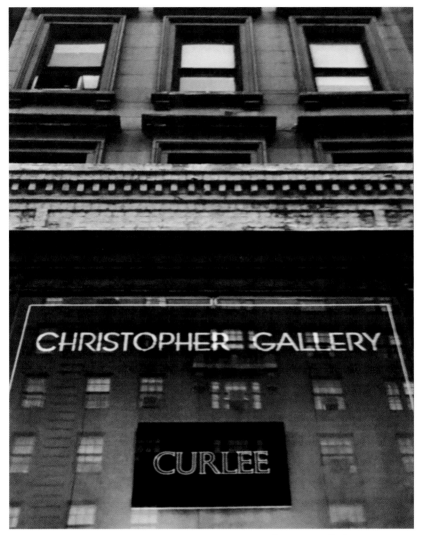

My debut as a professional artist with a solo exhibition at Christopher Gallery on Madison Avenue, New York City, October 1973.

award-winning menswear designer; John, who eventually wrote a best-selling novel; and Barry, the manager of a British rock star. Two of my very best friends from that era were Frank Cioffi and Joe Bonanno, a pair of Italian Americans from Brooklyn. They were gym boys, trim and buff. Frank was a Navy veteran who was a high-school history teacher. He had a tattoo decades before they were fashionable. Joe worked in an office in the World Trade Center. He had a famous last name—one of his relatives was a well-known mafia boss, a real-life godfather. Joe and Frank were best buddies, not boyfriends, and they were a bit older than me. For some reason, they took me—a relatively naive southern boy—under their wing as a project, and introduced me for the first time to the fairly new underground disco scene. We had many great Saturday nights together out on the town. They knew lots of people, and my circle of acquaintances grew larger.

I met another Douglas. Doug Capasso approached me on the street one day to compliment me on my crew cut. He was a stocky Italian American, just my age, and a bit rough looking until he smiled. Then his face lit up and I swear, his eyes actually sparkled. So did his personality. He was popular—people were drawn to him because he was so happy and positive. He had the knack of being the life of any party. I was totally smitten. Doug liked me right back, and soon we were officially boyfriends. He even got a crew cut like mine. We didn't move in together, but we spent most evenings at his apartment in the Village because he lived alone, and I didn't. It was cozy, and he actually had a fireplace—a rarity in New York. Doug was the owner of a temporary employment agency called Good People. The life of a freelancer can be precarious financially, but whenever I needed to make some extra money, Doug simply slotted me into a temporary secretarial job for as long as I needed—one of my perks as his boyfriend. Doug and I were very happy together for a couple of years, but eventually he fell in with some people I didn't like, began abusing cocaine, cheated on me, and broke my heart. Doug Capasso was my first real love, and I was devastated. It took a long time to get over it. But then, after a few long months of mooning over love lost, I had some help.

His name was Robert Cromwell. He was a burly Black fellow with a wide-open baby face. I had seen him around the Village and thought he was great-looking. One evening in the spring of 1976 when I was out with Frank and Joe, Robert and I connected. We were immediately drawn to one another. Five years older than me, Robert was dean of students at the Borough of Manhattan Community College. Besides being a real hunk, he was good-natured, kind, gentle, and loving. He was from Ohio and had moved to NYC from the sticks, just as I had. Robert was very social, made friends easily, and seemed to know everyone in the Village scene. I was far more reserved, and I admired and envied his ease with people. We quickly became an item. Robert was big, handsome, and affable. People liked him, and I was proud to be associated with him. Even better, he was smart. He was fun. He really liked me. I really liked him. I wasn't sad anymore.

Robert Cromwell, Los Angeles, 1978.

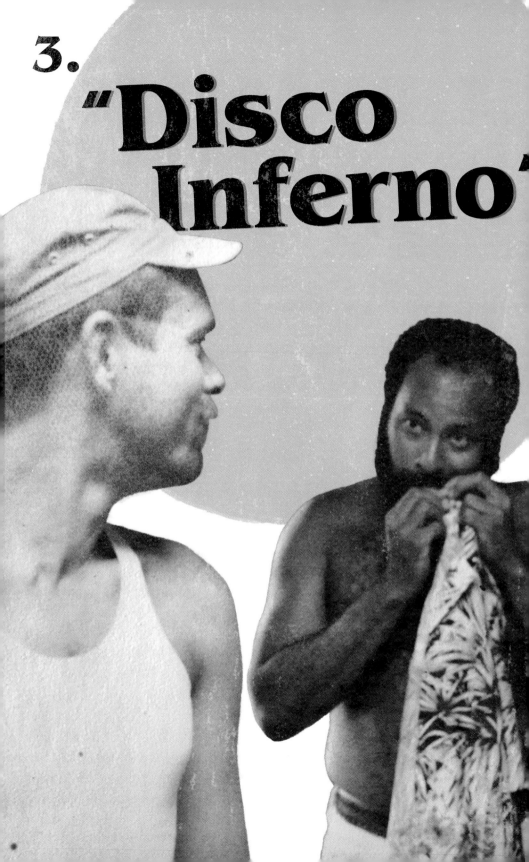

3.
"Disco Inferno"

A few weeks after we met, Robert and I experienced together one of the greatest events of that entire era. The Bicentennial of the United States was July 4th, 1976. On all of planet Earth, the place to be that day was Greenwich Village. It was a sunny day—hot, hazy, and humid. The West Side waterfront was thronged with thousands of people, there to see the magnificent flotilla of tall ships from all over the world sail up the Hudson River. The entire Village became one gigantic, raucous street party that lasted all day and late into the night. Robert lived in a big apartment on West 12th Street in the Village with an amazing view of Lower Manhattan and the World Trade Center. After dark we watched a spectacular fireworks display over New York Harbor from the rooftop of his building. I had already met Robert's best friend and roommate, Roger Blackmon, a shy, quiet Vietnam veteran who was an office manager as well as a talented amateur DJ. Now I met his other friends. Robert was one of a close-knit group of gay Black guys who gradually accepted me, a good southern white boy and now Robert's boyfriend, into their circle of friends. I introduced Joe and Frank, my disco buddies, to my new friends, and for the next couple of years we all hung out a lot in Robert and Roger's apartment. Roger had a complete DJ setup with dual turntables, and his music was always playing. We got stoned, partied, listened to music, and went out dancing on Saturday nights.

Me and Robert Cromwell at Fire Island Pines,
New York, 1978.

The first discotheques in the early 1960s were small nightclubs such as the Peppermint Lounge and Arthur's, catering to the jet set and celebrities. Instead of live bands for dancing, DJs spun records. In the early 1970s, a few entrepreneurs in New York took the idea and expanded it into large venues that could hold hundreds of people. Their DJs adopted the technique of mixing records on dual turntables to produce a continuous stream of music. One song blended seamlessly into the next, so the music played for hours without a single break. A talented DJ could take you on a journey—playing off the mood of the crowd, working it up into a frenzy, then backing off, again and again throughout an entire night. By 1975–76 there were several of these clubs in downtown Manhattan. They were not bars. They served no alcohol, just juice and water, so most people took recreational drugs to enhance the experience. They didn't advertise. The entrance was usually an unmarked door in a nonresidential neighborhood. If you were not part of the scene, you didn't even know that they existed. But once inside, you found yourself in a dark, cavernous space with flashing strobe lights, whirling mirrored disco balls, gigantic speakers blasting an unending series of songs with a continuous pounding beat, and hundreds of people losing themselves in a kind of collective, communal, euphoric revelry.

The dancing went on for many hours, usually from around midnight on Saturday night until midmorning on Sunday. Clubs like 12-West (in an old warehouse) and Flamingo (on the second floor of a bank building) were almost exclusively gay, while the Loft (the DJ's actual residence) and Paradise Garage (in an old garage building) attracted a mix of gay and straight, men and women, Black, white, and Latinx. Some were basically open to anyone for the price of admission, while others were only for members and their guests. But they all were places where people went to be part of something unique and, at its best, something cathartic and inspiring. *Saturday Night Fever,* the definitive disco movie from 1977 staring John Travolta, and the ultra famous Studio 54 were showbizzy versions of disco that came a bit later in a blaze of publicity after the media discovered the scene. Studio 54 was fun, and a fantastic place for people-watching, but the earlier, relatively secret underground clubs were the real deal.

A disco Saturday night usually began with a nap after a light dinner. Late in the evening, around eleven or midnight, a group of friends would gather at someone's apartment, socialize for a while, and prepare for the night ahead with alcohol and/or drugs. By the time you and your friends arrived at the chosen club at around one or two in the morning, the party had long since cranked up. Early in the night the music tended to be fast and driving, encouraging energetic, nonstop dancing. People wore jeans and boots, and after a while most guys removed their shirts and stuffed them into their back pockets. People took breaks to hit the juice bar, or share a joint while they socialized. When a particularly popular song came up in the mix, everyone raced back onto the crowded dance floor. As the night wore on, a good DJ would gradually soften their choices of music and slow down the frantic pace.

By around five or six in the morning, the crowd had typically thinned out, leaving room for the regulars to take over the club for what was called *sleaze*—dancing to great, and sometimes rare and obscure, R&B and soul classics that were completely different in tone and mood from the driving disco tunes of the early evening. The *hard core* were those people who were there every week for the sleaze hours, who recognized one another by sight, and who expected to see, acknowledge, and party with those same people every weekend, even if you may never have actually met outside the club. The night gradually ended by midmorning on Sunday as the last exhausted stragglers left the club in broad daylight, went home, and slept the day away, recovering from the intensity of the experience to resume their regular daily lives during the week ahead. By participating in the underground disco scene, you felt part of something really special—an amazing community of like-minded, nonjudgmental people who had a big, wonderful secret.

Coming right on the heels of Gay Liberation and Gay Pride, the experience of the early disco years gave thousands of out-and-proud urban gay men a palpable sense of cohesion and community. And disco gave people who may have struggled with their sexuality the opportunity actually to celebrate it along with hundreds of other beautiful young men, crowded together on a hot steamy dance floor

Sunday morning pre-dawn at Paradise Garage disco, New York City, late 1970s.

with their shirts off, slick with sweat and transported by great music. The disco was a place where, as a gay man, you *belonged*. Everyone who was there remembers it as a kind of golden era . . . before disaster struck.

* * *

By the last half of the 1970s, the social lives of many urban gay men revolved around sex, drugs, and disco. The Sexual Revolution, combined with the political movement of Gay Liberation, encouraged a frame of mind in which promiscuity was now the norm. It was easy to find partners for casual hookups, and many people had

multiple friends-with-benefits. Traditional European-style bath-houses had been part of urban gay life for decades, but now other, more raunchy sex clubs sprang up, where men went specifically for anonymous encounters. Many gay men embraced sexual freedom as a way of life. For some, easy casual sex became an addiction, offering a kind of release after years of repression and shame. For better or worse, drugs were part of it: weed, speed, cocaine, downers, LSD—all were cheap and readily available. Saturday nights were reserved for disco, and it became a weekly ritual, like going to church. In Edgar Allan Poe's famous story "The Masque of the Red Death", the revelers thought that they were safe from pestilence and plague behind thick castle walls. No one was aware that Death was already inside. Just as no one was aware that a dark specter was lurking in the shadows of the urban gay scene. HIV had crashed the party, and it was spreading, silent, invisible, and deadly.

Robert Cromwell and I had started as a red-hot romance, but eventually and gradually we settled into a profoundly rewarding, close friendship. Like my roommate Doug, Robert was a soul mate. Every summer he and his group of close friends rented a house in Fire Island Pines. Fire Island is a barrier island off the southern coast of Long Island—a big sand bar, really. Merely fifty miles from Manhattan, it is accessible only by ferry, and there are no cars. Houses are tucked in among the dunes and connected by a network of boardwalks. There are two Fire Island communities about a half-mile apart that are predominately gay. Cherry Grove had been a funky haven for sexually unconventional men and women for several decades. Then, beginning in the late 1960s and early '70s, the newer and more upscale Pines became a summer community primarily of affluent gay men. Once there, you were part of what seemed a gay paradise, completely removed from the real world. Many accomplished and famous gay New Yorkers had summer homes there.

The atmosphere was free and easy, very sexual, and very heady. Joe and Frank had first introduced me to the Pines in 1975. We went back several times that summer. For the next two years, as Robert's boyfriend, I was his houseguest most summer weekends. And then in 1978, when we were no longer romantically involved, he asked if I would like to officially join his summer household of good friends and take a share. There were six of us—Robert, Roger, Carl Johnson, Gordon Wilkins, Jay Collins, and me. Today the Pines is astronomically expensive, but in 1978 we each paid $1,000 to rent our house for the entire season. I was just beginning a new series of large paintings, so I took my work with me and set up shop for the summer. I lived there full time from May until October that year. During the week it was slow and quiet, and I worked, but on Friday afternoons hundreds of weekenders arrived on the ferries. Most of my city disco friends were there, and I met many new people. Besides Saturday nights at the Ice Palace disco, we enjoyed lazy days on the beach and elaborate theme parties. That summer our house threw a party called *Midnight Sleaze*. Roger worked his magic on the turntables all night long. It was *fabulous*, a trendy word we overused often in those days. I have two good friends, Nicholas and Richard, who first met at that party, fell in love, and are still together today after forty-five years. All my housemates were easygoing and relaxed. Already friends, we respected and really *liked* one another—a summer together made us almost like a family. We had so much fun. Little did we know that Fire Island Pines would become ground zero in the crisis to come.

On July 4th weekend in 1978, an old college buddy of Robert's came to visit for a week, and Robert brought him to the Pines. John Martin was from Los Angeles. He was hunky and cute, serious and intelligent. We really hit it off, and after the weekend and a night at the Ice Palace, he ended up staying with me in the Pines for the week while my housemates went back to the city. Besides the physical attraction, we bonded over a love of classical music, which was unusual in a social world dominated by disco. Robert was amused by my little romance with his old friend, but it soon became more than a fling for me. If you believe in love at first sight (and I do, since it had happened to me a couple of times before), this was it, big time.

After John went home, he and I kept in close touch. At the end of October, Robert and I flew to California. It was my first visit to the West Coast. We spent a few days in San Francisco, then we took the air shuttle to Los Angeles and stayed with John for a weekend. The spark was still there, stronger than ever. I secretly went back to visit John again for the long Thanksgiving weekend. I told no one, not even Doug Peix. My friends thought I went home to visit my family. I was seriously considering a major life change, and I needed to be certain. And in fact, during this visit John and I made the big decision to join our lives together. John was the circulation accounting manager for the *Los Angeles Times*. At thirty years old, he was successful, stable, and mature. I was now thirty-one and eager to finally settle down with the right person. Since John was a corporate guy and I was a freelancer, I could move and he could not. So I decided to leave New York.

My friends simply could not believe it. Robert was appalled and tried to talk me out of it. Although our sexual relationship had ended and we were not boyfriends anymore, we cared deeply for one another. He was hurt and felt responsible for what he considered to be a big mistake, but I had made up my mind. I got a gig with a shipping service to drive someone's car from New York to its owner in California. I only had to pay for the gas. Doug saw me off early one morning at the end of January 1979. It was snowing lightly. We hugged and said our goodbyes. We had been best friends for nine years. I watched him wave in the rearview mirror as I drove away. I am not an impulsive person, and it had been a wrenching decision. I didn't move because I wanted to leave New York. I went forward to a new life in Los Angeles because it felt right. I followed my heart and my gut in the biggest gamble I ever made. It was the end of my young manhood, and the beginning of a new stage of life.

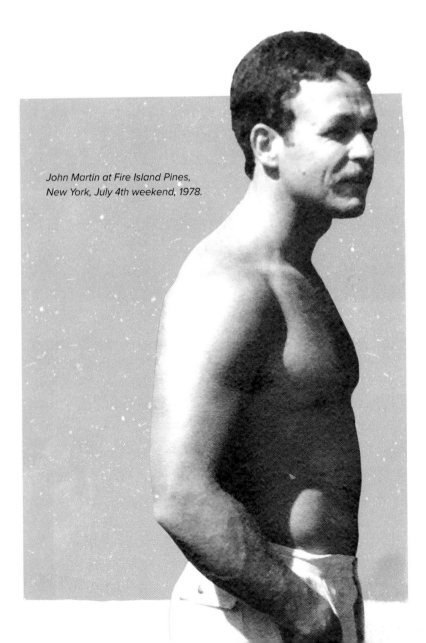

John Martin at Fire Island Pines, New York, July 4th weekend, 1978.

4.

"California Dreamin'"

I took the southern route to avoid winter weather and stopped off to visit my family in North Carolina. Of course I needed to explain to my parents why I was moving. We had never discussed my sexuality, but now I took the plunge. I was not surprised to find that they were not surprised. In my reserved southern family, things often were unspoken, but actually well understood. Whatever their questions might have been, my blue-collar dad and my housewife mom were totally supportive of me and my decisions, as they always had been. I was doing okay in life, I was happy, and that's what they wanted for me. It was my great good luck to have been their son. Many other young gay men are not so fortunate.

After nearly a week alone on the road, I arrived in Los Angeles right at the beginning of February 1979. For the last hundred miles on Interstate 10, the sun was slowly setting in the west, directly in front of me. It was dusk as I pulled up in John's driveway. After years in a small apartment, I would now be living in a house, with a yard and a dog. Maggie was a beautiful brindle Great Dane— golden with black tiger stripes, only a year old, and not quite yet fully grown. She bounded out, gave me a sniff, furiously wagged her tail, and leaned against me asking for some attention. She obviously remembered me from my visits a few months before. Because of

Starting a new life with John in California, 1979.

her size and her tiger stripes, Maggie looked intimidating, but she really was a big, sweet, overgrown puppy. John greeted me with a big bear hug and a kiss.

Now that I lived in California, I needed personal transportation. I hadn't had a car since college. John came up with a good plan. He sold me his Toyota station wagon, which was a few years old, and bought himself a little British sports car. A win-win situation.

It was hard at first. I missed New York and my friends desperately. Naturally enough, I was second-guessing my decision. Being a New Yorker was like a badge of honor, and it was harder than I thought it would be to give that up. For weeks my dreams were full of cubical buildings, and I was having a rough time of it. But Southern California is very seductive. The weather is wonderful. I loved John and he loved me. His friends took me into their lives, and gradually I came to love living in Los Angeles. In the beginning we went out dancing a few times, but the LA boys didn't have a clue. The intensity of the New York scene was missing. Instead of a profound communal ritual, an evening at an LA disco was just a bunch of men partying, and without my New York friends it was boring. John liked to go out partying once in a while, and soon once in a while was enough for me as well. That part of my life ended when I left New York, and soon I didn't miss the disco scene at all. In California there were many other interesting things to do.

Before the move I had wrapped up my business with my New York gallery and shipped all of my unsold paintings to California. I set up a new studio in our home, and soon I was hard at work again. I found a new gallery (owned by Faye Dunaway, the movie star!) and was back in business. A new life. A house and a car. A great relationship. A new group of friends. And even a dog. All was good.

During my New York years, I had rarely ever left Manhattan, except for the time I spent on Fire Island or an annual trip home for the holidays with my family in North Carolina. Now John and I visited Las Vegas, San Diego, San Francisco, and Palm Springs. We traveled to Grand Canyon. We went camping in the wilderness north of Los Angeles. In 1981 we took a road trip up the spectacular Pacific Coast Highway in John's little MGB sports car to Seattle for the annual Wagner opera festival. We came back home through Crater Lake and Yosemite National Parks. Most, but not all, of our friends were gay, but eventually we had very little to do with the local gay scene, except for an occasional night out for a couple of beers in a gay bar. John even had a piano, and for the first time since I had left home for college, I began practicing and playing again for my own pleasure.

I loved it when my New York friends came to Los Angeles. After a few months had passed, Robert realized that my commitment to John was real and serious. He let me know that he was happy for us, and he was the first of many to visit. During the summer of 1981, my good friend and disco buddy Frank Cioffi visited. Since he was a teacher, he had time off and ended up staying for most of the summer. We put him up in our guest room, and he got a part-time job as a bouncer in a lesbian bar. John was cool and relaxed about it, and I loved having Frank around for a few months. He had never been to LA before, and we had a great time. We were good friends before, and after a summer spent in the same house, we were great friends now. I was sorry to see him go back to New York at the end of the summer.

✱✱✱

Early in 1981 Robert called to tell me that someone we knew had died. Enno Poersch and Nick Rock were a prominent couple in the Fire Island community. I knew them only socially from parties and disco nights, but Robert was good friends with Enno and knew them quite well. Nick had been sick for a few months. Then he began wasting away. He was hospitalized with a virulent brain infection and then had a heart attack. Soon his organs were failing. Nick was dying and the doctors didn't know why. He was put on life support and lapsed into a coma. When all hope was gone, Enno and Nick's sister made the decision to let him die. Robert was particularly troubled by this news—he told me there were rumors that a few other men from Fire Island were sick with similar symptoms and someone else had also died.

RARE CANCER SEEN IN 41 HOMOSEXUALS

Outbreak Occurs Among Men in New York and California—8 Died Inside 2 Years.

—*New York Times*, Friday, July 3, 1981

In June 1981 the Centers for Disease Control published a report that five otherwise healthy gay men in LA had developed a rare lung infection, and that two had died. This news was followed by reports of a few gay men with a rare and unusually aggressive cancer in both New York and California. On July 3 the *New York Times* published an alarming article titled "Rare Cancer Seen in 41 Homosexuals." By the end of 1981, a total of 270 cases of the mysterious illness had been reported, and 121 people had died.

In California I still subscribed to the *New York Times*. I vividly recall coming across the article titled "Rare Cancer Seen in 41 Homosexuals," and feeling a shiver of alarm. Coming only a few months after Nick's death, this article was the very first official inkling the general public had that something bad was happening. Like distant thunder, these outbreaks were the rumblings of the disaster to come. Doctors knew that the immune systems of these men had failed, allowing the rare conditions to take hold, but otherwise they were mystified. The outbreaks were becoming an epidemic. Researchers called the condition GRID—Gay-Related Immune Deficiency. Robert's Fire Island friend Nick Rock had been among the very first to die of the mysterious illness.

John's employer, the *Los Angeles Times*, also owned a magazine company called Times Mirror. They needed a new controller (head of the accounting department), and during the summer of 1982, John was offered the job. This was a big promotion, a real step up in his corporate career. Of course he accepted the offer. But Times Mirror was based in New York. He was eager to move, but at first I was conflicted. By now I had been in California for three and a half years, and we had a good life in LA. But once I really thought about returning to my old friends and the great city that I loved, I was all in. John made an advance trip back east to find an apartment. He came up with a nice big loft in an old factory building on West 37th Street and brought home photos for my approval. The next couple of months were a whirlwind. We sold the house and bought the loft. I supervised packing and made shipping arrangements while John flew to New York to start his new job. In early October 1982, I drove across the country once more, this time with Maggie to keep me company. She rode curled up in the front seat beside me with the rest of the car packed solid with stuff. I snuck her into motel rooms at night during the trip. When I arrived in Manhattan and saw the loft in person, I was thrilled. We were on the eleventh floor and had a spectacular, close-up view of midtown Manhattan. After nearly four years in California, I was back home in New York, only in a committed relationship with a solid life partner, a much better apartment, and more money. And of course, a very large dog.

Me and Maggie,
Los Angeles, 1980.

5.
Gay Cancer

Good friendships are priceless. I was able to pick right back up where we had left off with most of my New York friends. Doug Peix now had a partner, too, both in life and in business. He was a young architect named William Crawford, but everyone called him Metro. Together they had started their own architectural firm. Robert Cromwell now had a boyfriend named David McDiarmid, who was an artist from Sydney, Australia. Apparently Robert had a thing for artists! Frank Cioffi and Joe Bonanno were still great fun to hang out with. My former Pines housemates were happy that I was back, and all of my old friends quickly became friends with John. He was easy to like. George Shechtman, owner of my former gallery, welcomed me back into his stable of artists. He had closed the Madison Avenue location and moved to SoHo, a trendy neighborhood of loft buildings and art galleries. Doug and Metro had designed a big, gorgeous space for exhibiting paintings in the new location. George renamed his business Gallery Henoch. I was thrilled when he offered me a tenth-anniversary one-man show for autumn 1983. It felt good to be back in New York.

Me, Gordon Wilkins, and Roger Blackmon,
former Fire Island housemates, New York City, 1980s.

It had not been as perceptible in sprawling LA, but in New York the atmosphere of gay life had changed. The golden age of the secret underground 1970s disco scene was done. A new downtown gay superclub called the Saint had opened in 1980. Known as the Vatican of Disco, it was a spectacular venue with a planetarium-style dome over the vast dance floor and an elaborate, high-tech lighting system. The Saint drew crowds of 2,500 people every weekend, and for big theme parties, it could hold as many as four thousand revelers. A $4.6 million renovation of the old Fillmore East theater of rock and roll fame, with an entrance right on 2nd Avenue, the Saint wasn't exactly underground or secret.

Everyone was still dancing and having casual sex, but at the same time there was an ominous, frantic undercurrent. It was terrifying that more and more gay men were getting sick, wasting away, and dying horrible, gruesome deaths. By now, a few straight people, both men and women, were getting sick as well. It was clear that the mysterious illness was not a disease limited to men who have sex with men. Accordingly, the acronym GRID was officially changed to AIDS—Acquired Immunodeficiency Syndrome. But to the general public, the disease was becoming known derisively as the *gay cancer*. The cause was unknown. No treatments seemed to work. All that was certain was that people were suffering and dying.

✴✴✴

During that first winter back in New York, it was wonderful to see John become a real New Yorker. He loved his job. I think he liked being the boss. His office was on Park Avenue at 32nd Street, about a mile from the loft. He enjoyed walking to work in nice weather. With no yard, Maggie needed three or four walks every day—a bit of an adjustment after simply opening a door and letting her out in California. She was a very intelligent dog and learned the new routine quickly. Great Danes are rare in New York, so she got lots of attention when we took her out.

The loft was one big, open space with high ceilings and enormous windows, an open kitchen at one end, and a bathroom. Doug and Metro designed for us a raised bedroom area with a crawl space for storage underneath and a big walk-in closet with a guest sleeping loft above. For the very first time I had a big, proper studio setup flooded with north light. Between other paintings I was working intermittently on a very ambitious series of twenty paintings of nineteenth-century Wagnerian opera singers. I had begun the series in 1978 in the Pines, and I still had a couple of years of work until completion.

Doug and Metro now lived and ran their business in a loft on lower Fifth Avenue at Madison Square. Our good friends Gail and Michael lived and operated their ad agency in the same building. Doug and I had both come a long way from our small apartment in Little Italy, and Gail and Michael's business was thriving and now had some major clients. The six of us all celebrated Christmas together that year and began a long tradition of having an elaborate holiday dinner together every year. John and I gave one another cutting-edge gadgets—an early personal IBM computer and a CD player. The primitive computer was good only for spreadsheets and word processing, but the CD player was great. Now we could listen to Mozart, Beethoven, and Brahms without the annoying pops and scratches that were inevitable with vinyl LPs.

Over the months we settled into a routine. We both were concentrating on our careers. Gay people could not be officially married then, but otherwise we were exactly like a married couple. Our social life centered on having people over, going out to dinner with friends, or attending the occasional concert or Broadway show.

With the epidemic ramping up, we felt very lucky to be living in a committed relationship outside of the sexual fray of the promiscuous gay scene.

✻✻✻

Nick Rock had died in January 1981. By the end of 1982, 772 cases of AIDS and 618 deaths had been recorded, primarily in New York, San Francisco, and Los Angeles—the centers of gay culture in the United States. It was becoming clear that this was just the tip of an immense iceberg. Federal health officials were estimating that tens of thousands of people might be walking around with the disease without knowing they were carrying it; they had no symptoms—yet. The growing realization that it was just beginning was horrifying.

The first heterosexuals in the United States to be diagnosed with AIDS were intravenous drug users—both men and women. At first this seemed to support a theory that the condition was caused by tainted drugs, since many urban gay men used recreational drugs. But then, most alarmingly to the medical establishment, a few people suffering from hemophilia became ill. Hemophilia is a genetically determined, life-threatening condition that prevents blood from clotting properly. It is controlled through replacement therapy using a blood product called clotting factor, which is manufactured from donated blood and then introduced intravenously into a hemophiliac's bloodstream. Since the AIDS patients with hemophilia were not gay men or drug users, it was clear that the donated blood itself was infected with something that caused the disease. It followed that AIDS was spread between intravenous drug users through the common practice of sharing needles.

With the increasingly dire news about the epidemic that was now all around us, John and I just kept our heads down and got on with life. Early in 1983, friends from California came to visit. Tim Bennett and Bill Hunter had been John's good friends for a long

Up until now, AIDS had been dismissed by most politicians and even many medical professionals as a problem only for homosexuals and drug addicts. They considered the so-called gay cancer a disease of outcasts and lowlifes, who got what they deserved for their degenerate lifestyle. But suddenly there was a stark new reality. If any part of the blood supply was tainted, then anyone who received a transfusion during an operation might be at risk for contracting AIDS. Their sexual orientation or drug use had nothing to do with it.

In March 1983 the Centers for Disease Control issued a new report stating that most cases of AIDS so far were in homosexual men with multiple sexual partners, people who injected street drugs, Haitians, and hemophiliacs. Why people from Haiti? No one knew. The report concluded that the most likely cause was an infectious agent transmitted sexually, or through contact with blood or blood products. Clearly, anyone might potentially be at risk. The stakes were raised sky-high. AIDS was rapidly becoming a public health crisis of the first magnitude. There were now also cases of AIDS in Europe. When an epidemic becomes widespread across countries and affects large portions of the population, it is considered a pandemic. A frantic, concentrated search was on for the infectious agent. Without knowing the cause, there could be no effective treatment, much less a cure. Research labs in France and the United States were competing for the discovery.

time, and after my years in California, now they were mine as well. Tim teasingly called me "The Artist." He was about five years older than the rest of us. He had married in the mid-1960s and had kids. In the early '70s, he struggled with his sexual identity, decided to be true to his real nature, and divorced his wife to be with Bill, all while continuing to be a good father to his children. Tim and Bill's home was in Laguna Beach, about an hour south of LA. They were corporate headhunters whose very specialized business was finding suitable candidates for positions in high-tech and scientific companies. Tim and Bill came to New York every month or so to interview applicants. Since we had plenty of space, we got into the routine of having them as guests. They would spend the weekend with us and then go to a hotel for a couple of days for their interviews. We enjoyed having them and looked forward to their visits. Tim and Bill were very social. They knew lots of people on both coasts. Over the next few years we hosted a few big parties together at the loft. We made several new friends through Tim and Bill. One of the most important of these was Joe Palmeri. They had known him for many years. Joe was a school administrator who lived in Queens. We socialized with him a lot and he became our very close friend.

Since Nick Rock's death, John and I didn't personally know anyone who was sick, but now it seemed that almost every gay man in New York knew, or at least knew about, someone with AIDS. Tim and Bill brought news of the epidemic from California. They knew several people who were ill. And the word was getting around about the true nature of the disease, and how utterly horrifying it was. The grim reality of the situation was settling in.

May 20, 1983

The Pasteur Institute in Paris reported the discovery of a retrovirus that could be the cause of AIDS. They called it LAV.

September 1983

The Centers for Disease Control had reported that HIV can be present in blood, or in certain body fluids—semen, vaginal secretions, rectal secretions, and breast milk. It can be passed between sexes, and to a baby if a person is pregnant. But the virus is not present in sweat, tears, mucus, or saliva. At last it was proved that HIV is not spread by casual contact, food, water, air, or environmental surfaces.

April 23, 1984

Researchers at the National Cancer Institute announced they had confirmed the cause of AIDS—a retrovirus labeled HTLV-III.

The competition between these two laboratories was fierce. At stake were millions of research dollars, not to mention the credit and fame for the discovery. It turned out that both had found the same virus. The French were first to isolate it, and the Americans verified it with proof. After a big controversy lasting several years, in the end the credit was shared. The virus finally was called Human Immunodeficiency Virus, or HIV.

Acquired Immunodeficiency Syndrome is a chronic condition in which a person's immune system is damaged and gradually fails. This allows an array of infections and diseases potentially to take hold. As the disease progresses, more and more infections pile on so that several different diseases or infections might be ravaging the body all at once. Different people have different opportunistic infections, so the course of the disease varies from person to person.

In the beginning the symptoms are often fever, fatigue, diarrhea, weight loss, shingles (an extremely painful form of herpes zoster, also known as chickenpox, which can appear anywhere on the body), and thrush, an oral yeast infection that causes a thick white coating on the tongue.

Next is a progression to full-blown AIDS with symptoms such as bed-drenching night sweats, chills, recurring fevers, chronic diarrhea, swollen lymph glands, white spots or lesions in the mouth, and persistent, unexplained fatigue and weakness.

AIDS patient Deotis McMather at the San Francisco General AIDS ward, 1983. After his AIDS diagnosis, he returned home to find his belongings on the street.

Then major infections begin. They can include *Pneumocystis jirovecii* (PCP) pneumonia, a rare form of pneumonia caused by a common fungus; tuberculosis; cytomegalovirus, which can damage the eyes, digestive tract, lungs, or other organs; meningitis, a dangerous inflammation of the membranes surrounding the brain; toxoplasmosis, a parasite that causes heart disease and which can cause seizures when present in the brain; lymphoma, a cancer of the blood; and Kaposi's sarcoma (KS), a normally rare, virulent cancer of the blood vessel wall. KS usually appears as red or purple lesions on the skin and in the mouth, but the lesions can appear anywhere on the body.

There is more.

The end stages can include wasting syndrome (extreme weight loss), kidney failure, liver failure, and neurological complications—confusion, forgetfulness, depression, difficulty walking, behavioral changes, and reduced mental functioning that results in severe dementia, weakness, blindness, and the inability to function.

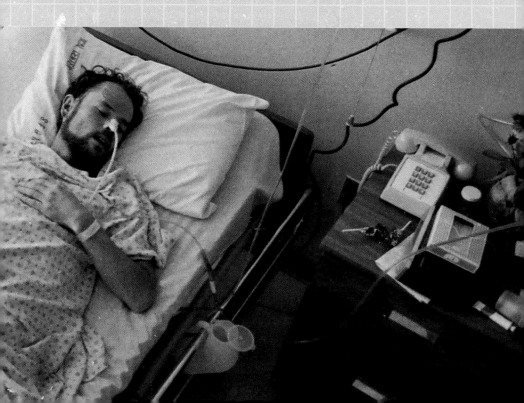

6.
America Reacts

Activists participate in a candlelight vigil honoring the dead at Hyde Park, Sydney, Australia, 1993.

My ten-year retrospective show was in October 1983. It was a real thrill to see old and new paintings filling the beautiful new gallery space. All my friends came to the opening. Some of them had been there at the beginning of my career, but many of the earlier paintings were new to my more recent friends, and the California paintings were new to almost everyone. Afterward, Robert; his boyfriend, David; and my other Pines housemates took John and me to Jezebel, a restaurant in Hell's Kitchen, near the loft. It was Black-owned and served authentic soul food in an elaborately romantic southern environment. Recently opened, the restaurant was a hit, drawing both the foodie and theater crowds. The eight of us had

a big round table near the center of the room. It was a wonderful night to remember—celebrating my professional life publicly at the gallery, and privately with dear old friends.

The United States was beginning to react to AIDS. From the beginning of the epidemic, religious conservatives were railing against the "godless" homosexuals, who had brought down the terrible Wrath of the Almighty upon their own heads. Homophobia was much more acceptable and pervasive in the early 1980s than today—it was the default position of a great majority of people. Most big city gay people were liberated and lived their lives openly by now, but in the rest of America—not so much. And now the stigma of "gay cancer" had taken hold. Before the HIV virus was discovered, people were afraid, because no one knew exactly how the disease was spread. People with AIDS were regarded in the same way as lepers in the Bible, to be shunned as "unclean." A New York doctor was threatened with eviction from his building for treating AIDS patients, prompting the first AIDS discrimination lawsuit. The certainty that HIV was not spread by casual contact was very important news.

By now isolated AIDS cases were cropping up all over America. Gay men from smaller towns and cities who traveled to New York or San Francisco and had sex there took the virus back home with them. And not only gay men. Obviously, men who identify as bisexual were at risk, but in addition, many men who adamantly identify as straight have occasional same-sex encounters. The married businessman from Peoria who came to New York for work and had a couple of nights out on the town and engaged in a casual gay hookup risked infecting his wife as well as himself.

***

AIDS brought out the worst in some people. Conservative politicians made lewd jokes about the situation. (Two examples: What do you call a straight man with AIDS? A liar. What's the hardest part about getting AIDS? Convincing your parents that you're Haitian.) There were ever more and more sick young men who had lost their jobs, or had been evicted from their apartments, or whose parents had disowned them. There were those who cared for their life

At first the medical establishment circled warily around AIDS. The doctors and nurses actually treating patients were in the vanguard, but research money lagged, with homophobia even in the medical community as a contributing factor. Since no one knew exactly how the disease was spread, a few medical professionals refused to treat AIDS patients for fear of becoming infected themselves. San Francisco General Hospital was the first to have a special ward for AIDS, staffed by volunteers. It filled up quickly with dying men and established the standard of care that was soon adopted by other hospitals.

AIDS became a political football, just as COVID-19 has. San Francisco had a large percentage of people who are gay (and still does), so the gay community there had real political clout. The push in Congress for more AIDS funding was organized by Democratic Californian politicians. But ex-movie actor Republican Ronald Reagan had become president in January 1981, right at the moment when people started dying. Conservative Republicans were in charge in Washington. They tried as much as possible to ignore AIDS. Their political allies, conservative Christians (the so-called Moral Majority) loudly denounced homosexuality. The atmosphere was hostile, with pervasive institutionalized homophobia inhibiting fundraising and progress in what should have been recognized as a public health issue.

partners until homophobic relatives swooped in and cut them out. If a gay couple had not arranged their affairs legally, when one died, his relatives might contest an inheritance, in spite of the actual wishes of the deceased. Many people with AIDS were treated as pariahs. Some funeral homes even refused to handle the bodies of the dead.

But AIDS also brought out the best in others. In the gay community, after the initial shock of what we were facing sank in, people began organizing. Thirty years of gay political activism, beginning tentatively in the 1950s and increasing during the liberation movements of the 1960s and early 1970s, had produced real results in the form of Gay Pride and visibility. But the unfolding horror of the AIDS crisis inspired a new, more focused and urgent kind of activism that attracted many new people—fear for one's own life and the lives of one's friends was a powerful motivator. One of the first and most important of the new activist organizations in New York was the Gay Men's Health Crisis, founded in 1982 by a group of affluent gay men who knew one another from Fire Island Pines. It is a nonprofit information conduit and charitable operation that raises funds for research and provides crisis counseling and legal aid. When GMHC opened a hotline, they received more than one hundred calls the first day. Other similar organizations sprang up in San Francisco and LA.

A group of AIDS activists in San Francisco organized a candlelight march from the predominantly gay Castro District to city hall on May 2, 1983. New York activists picked up the idea and organized their own march for the same day. As they marched they were joined by thousands of people, of all sexualities, putting a human face to the crisis for the first time. Over the next several months, memorial marches and services were held across America in which thousands participated. In the nation's capital, a candlelight procession by the White House was joined by 1,300 people on October 8.

AIDS activists march to City Hall, San Francisco, May 2, 1983.

Within the gay community, there was increasing controversy about personal responsibility. Calls for closing sex clubs, bathhouses, and other places that encouraged anonymous encounters—many coming from within the gay male community—were met by other gay men with a certain amount of hostility. People who had grown up in more repressed times considered their sexual freedom to be hard-won, and, naturally enough, resisted the idea that this freedom be regulated. Safe-sex campaigns began around this time. Certain sexual activities are riskier than others, and condoms can block the exchange of semen that carries the virus. But certain voices within the gay community acknowledged that AIDS was spread very efficiently by rampant promiscuity, and that something needed to be done. Encouraging safe sex or providing educational information in the sex clubs was all very well and good, but the clubs were obviously incubators of the virus. As horrible as it seems, there were even rumors that people with early stage

AIDS, bitter about their situation, were going out to the clubs to deliberately infect other men. In retrospect, it was a no-brainer. San Francisco was first to close the sex clubs, but soon New York and LA cracked down as well.

✳ ✳ ✳

March 2, 1985

The first commercial blood test to detect HIV antibodies was approved by the Food and Drug Administration. It was meant for screening the US blood supply, not as a diagnostic test. Many gay men rejected the idea of being tested out of hand. Since there was no treatment available for AIDS, much less a cure, the knowledge of infection seemed to many a heavier burden to carry than the simple fear of not knowing. Also, the political climate was generally hostile, and many men were afraid of landing on a database that might be used against them in the future. After all, some influential conservatives on the far right-wing fringe were calling for compulsory tattoos or even forced quarantine of people with AIDS in internment camps! There was a constant pushback to this overt repression from established gay-rights organizations as well as grassroots movements.

The 1984 Olympic Games were held in Los Angeles. Doug and Metro flew to California that summer with John and me. Metro was an accomplished amateur gymnast. He had even installed a pair of gymnast's rings hanging from the high ceiling of their loft, so he was particularly interested in those events. We all stayed with one of our best LA friends, Richard Gillmore, an automotive executive who lived in Hollywood. It was Doug's first trip to California, and I really enjoyed showing him the sprawling city.

In October the gallery exhibited my German opera singers: twenty life-sized paintings with a total of thirty figures—the cast of Richard Wagner's Ring cycle of operas. Burly men and hefty women pose in costumes with winged helmets, armor, swords, and shields from the original production in 1876. I had been planning and then working on this complex series of large paintings for more than five years. There was an additional painting in a separate alcove, a portrait of the Police, one of the great rock bands of the 1980s. It was commissioned by their manager as a potential album cover, but then the band broke up and there were no more albums. Win some. Lose some.

President Reagan was reelected in November that year. In national politics AIDS was scarcely ever mentioned. The media only paid close attention when someone "innocent," meaning *not* gay, was affected. A hemophiliac, or perhaps a mother who received a transfusion during an operation would receive sympathetic coverage in the media, while the Moral Majority and other homophobic religious and cultural conservatives had the attitude that gay people and drug addicts who had AIDS somehow deserved it.

7.

The Summer of 1985

Late that spring in Laguna Beach, Tim Bennett and Bill Hunter were part of a group of friends and neighbors who organized an AIDS fundraising event. It was a poolside extravaganza with silly skits and a clumsy, comic water ballet, featuring burly men in matching Speedos, bathing caps, and tutus. John and I flew out to California for the Big Splash. We stayed with Tim and Bill. Their neighbors Al Roberts and Ken Jillson were the main organizers and hosts for the show—the stage was their deck and pool while Tim and Bill's house right next door was the backstage area. The Big Splash was a smash hit in the local gay community and got lots of publicity. It became an annual event. Over a period of twenty-four years the event got bigger and more professional, with Hollywood talent participating, and ultimately, over time, it raised a total of nearly ten million dollars for AIDS research and community assistance for local people with AIDS. This was only one example of the altruism of the gay community rallying around the common cause.

The first Big Splash fundraiser, Laguna Beach, California, 1985.

The Big Splash was great fun, but at the end of the trip we had some terrible news. Before flying home, we went to LA to see John's ex-partner, Ed Krisher. They had been together for about five years, but eventually grew apart and had split up about a year before I met John. But they remained good friends, and during my LA years, Ed became my good friend, too. Over dinner he told us haltingly that his doctor had given him the bad news that he was in the beginning phase of AIDS. Ed was a big strapping guy with a great body, and he certainly didn't look sick. But now he was, and he was frightened. John was beside himself. He had loved Ed, and still cared for him as a dear friend. Suddenly, at a stroke, AIDS was personal and in our faces. It was a somber flight home.

That summer we rented a vacation house on the North Fork of Long Island, a beautiful rural area with small villages, beaches, farms, and vineyards about two hours from Manhattan. Both Doug and Metro and Gail and Michael had recently purchased second homes there, so we decided to give it a try. After a couple of summers in sweltering New York City without air-conditioning in the loft, the thought of weekends at the shore with good friends nearby sounded very appealing. We took a house with a view of Long Island Sound. I brought out supplies for work, and for most of the summer Maggie and I stayed there while John took the train out for long weekends and a two-week vacation around the Fourth of July.

✳ ✳ ✳

Late in August an AIDS story made the national news. Ryan White was a young teenager from Indiana who contracted AIDS through contaminated blood products used to treat his hemophilia. He had just turned fourteen when he was diagnosed. His local middle school barred him from attending his classes. His parents sued, and there was a very public and protracted legal battle over Ryan's right to attend school. There was no rational reason for barring him. It had already been proven that AIDS is not spread by casual day-to-day contact. Young Mr. White displayed remarkable courage and dignity, and he chose to speak out publicly. His touching story resonated nationwide with many of those who still thought of AIDS only as gay cancer. He was perceived as an innocent victim of the virus, and he became the face of AIDS education. "AIDS is not a gay disease," was the new watchword for AIDS organizers.

Although it was important news, Ryan White's story—which was only national news because he was *not* a gay man—barely registered with us. We were in crisis. AIDS had crashed headlong into our lives for real. One weekend, out on the North Fork sometime that August, Doug called one Saturday afternoon to let me know that they were going back to New York. Metro was feeling ill and wanted to be home in the city. The very next day he was admitted to the hospital with pneumonia. He was quickly placed in intensive care, then on life support, and then he died. It all happened within

Ryan White at a press conference, after going public with his diagnosis, August 1985.

a matter of days, maybe a week. None of us can really remember. We were all back in the city, and we were in shock. Gail and Michael and John and I visited Metro in the hospital soon after he was first admitted. That was the last time we saw him. Doug told me later Metro had a case of thrush, often an early symptom of AIDS, a few months before, and had gone to the doctor. There had been no other symptoms, and otherwise he seemed perfectly healthy. If Metro suspected that he had AIDS, he did not discuss it with Doug. Sometimes people misinterpreted or concealed their symptoms so their friends did not know. Perhaps he was in denial. Normally it takes months or years for AIDS to run its course. But in this case there was no time to prepare, or even think. Metro was fine. Then he was dead. Doug describes the experience as a "car wreck."

That was only the first part of the crisis. The sudden shock tipped Doug over some kind of edge. After Metro went into intensive care, Gail and I could tell that Doug was in a very bad place. He wasn't functioning properly. He was either frantically manic and couldn't sleep, or he was morbidly depressed. Right after Metro died, I stayed with Doug for a few nights to try and keep him centered and calm. Things only got worse, and it didn't take long to realize that it was time to get some help. It's a terrible thing to watch your best friend totally flip out. Gail found a psychiatrist, and together we convinced Doug that he needed professional help. He wasn't happy about it, but we reminded him that he had a business to run, and that it had been Metro's business, too. I went with Doug to the psychiatrist. Gail and I felt that my description of events would help the doctor understand what was happening. He prescribed medication, along with some therapy, and Doug's roller-coaster moods gradually evened out. After a few months had passed and things had settled down, there was a memorial service for Metro. A few people got up and spoke about him, and a soloist sang one of Richard Strauss's sublime *Four Last Songs*. Besides being an amateur gymnast, Metro Crawford had been an opera lover.

On September 27, 1985, Hurricane Gloria, a Category 1 storm, made landfall on eastern Long Island. We had intended to keep the rental house over the winter, but it was badly damaged in the storm, and was now unlivable—a fitting end to our tragic Long Island summer.

8.
Star Power

URGENT. ROCK HUDSON FATALLY ILL. URGENT.

Actor Rock Hudson, last of the traditional square-jawed, romantic leading men . . . is suffering from inoperable liver cancer possibly linked to AIDS, it was disclosed today.

—*United Press International*, Tuesday, July 23, 1985

Everyone in Hollywood knew that Rock Hudson was gay. It was common knowledge in the gay community as well. But for much of the homophobic American public, it was a shocking realization that the handsome, manly movie idol was homosexual. For the next few months, the coverage about his illness put AIDS squarely on the front pages. This ongoing story was the backdrop to our personal crisis.

A week before the press release, Rock Hudson had appeared at an event with Doris Day, one of his movie costars from the early

Rock Hudson, one of the most famous movie stars of the 1950s and 1960s, at the beginning of his career.

Rock Hudson and Doris Day, his famous costar and friend, during his last public appearance, Los Angeles, July 1985.

September 17, 1985

At a press conference in the midst of his friend Rock Hudson's final illness, President Ronald Reagan first uttered the word AIDS in public, in response to a question about AIDS funding. The epidemic was just breaking when Reagan first took office. Now, after five long years, he finally was forced to acknowledge it for the first time. By now more than twelve thousand Americans had contracted AIDS. More than one half of those were dead. There was no end in sight. And nearly two more years would pass before Reagan would finally make a policy speech about AIDS on May 31, 1987. The inaction of the conservative Reagan administration was infuriating to AIDS activists.

1960s. His gaunt, haggard appearance was alarming, and reporters were told that he had just recovered from the flu. Under the radar, Mr. Hudson had already been ill for a year. He had Kaposi's sarcoma, a type of cancer common in people with AIDS, and now he was also diagnosed with lymphoma. After this last public appearance, he went to Paris for treatment, but his condition deteriorated quickly. There were no more treatments available. There was nothing to be done but return to Los Angeles to die. A commercial airliner was chartered to take Mr. Hudson home. His arrival was met with a swarm of paparazzi. Someone managed to get a shot of a gurney with a wasted figure beneath a blanket. Throughout all of this there had been nothing but denials from his spokesman, but once back in the UCLA Medical Center, Rock Hudson finally allowed the truth to be told. He was critically ill with AIDS, but he was in the closet until the bitter end. He still never said explicitly that he was gay. He died on October 2, 1985.

The illness and death of a closeted movie star turned out to be a game changer. For the first time AIDS was front page news. The Rock Hudson coverage was extensive and ongoing. The media found different angles to explore during his last few months, and the entire process was a kind of education for America about the epidemic in their midst. AIDS activists were at once grateful for the concentrated attention at long last, but also angry that thousands of deaths had been ignored or dismissed before Rock Hudson's celebrity death.

The American Foundation for AIDS Research (amfAR), a brand-new organization, was jump-started by a donation of $250,000 from Rock Hudson's estate. His dear friend and fellow movie star Elizabeth Taylor became the chairperson and very public face of amfAR. When world-famous celebrities began taking up the cause, AIDS itself was out of the closet.

9.
An Era of Pain and Sorrow

For the first five years of the AIDS epidemic, until Metro died, John and I were not really personally affected. Like all urban gay men, we were afraid for our lives. Although the incubation period certainly varied by individual, we knew that a person might be infected with the virus for as long as ten years before becoming ill. We tried to stay healthy and to practice safe sex. John and I contributed to Gay Men's Health Crisis and participated in some fundraising events, but basically we tried to keep our focus on our careers and our life together. Early in 1986, John went to LA on business and visited Ed Krisher, only to find him in pretty bad shape. He had Kaposi's sarcoma and had been in the hospital with a bout of pneumonia. He was now back home with wasting syndrome. John came home dejected by Ed's wretched condition. It was clear that he was dying, with only a few more months to live.

Bill Hunter, Tim Bennett, and Joe Palmeri,
Laguna Beach, California, early 1980s.

That summer we rented another house on the North Fork and during the season searched for a house to buy for ourselves. My mom and dad came to New York to visit for a week around the long Labor Day weekend. Some of my work was hanging in a group show at the gallery, and I was proud to have my folks meet George, the gallery owner, and to see for themselves the professional person I had become. We went to see *A Chorus Line,* the hit Broadway musical, and John and I treated them to a really good, really expensive New York steakhouse. We took them out to the North Fork, where they had a great time. Gail and Michael had us over for lunch. Doug joined us and we all went out for an afternoon on the bay in their boat. It turned out to be a visit to remember. By then we had found a house we liked, and we sealed the deal while my parents were visiting. I was so happy my dad got to see it. Sadly, their visit was memorable for another reason. My dad died suddenly of a heart attack only three months later. I never saw him alive again.

The year 1986 was when the government finally started paying attention to AIDS. Over the strenuous objections of conservatives, US Surgeon General Dr. C. Everett Koop released a report stating that AIDS cannot be spread casually and calling for a nationwide education campaign, including early sex education in schools, increased use of condoms, and voluntary HIV testing. The National Institute of Health followed up with a call for a massive media, educational, and public health campaign to curb HIV infections as well as for the creation of the National Commission on AIDS. These were positive developments, but to many people it felt like too little, too late. Just as with the COVID-19 pandemic, so many good people had already died while the government flailed around and took no real action to help them.

We tried as best we could to live a normal life, but by now there was a constant, pervasive pall hanging over everything. More and more people were getting sick and dying. The relentless news of suffering and death took its toll. Fire Island Pines had been ground zero for the epidemic in New York, with the first cluster of AIDS cases spreading from there. The Pines community from the '70s was gradually decimated. Many of the casual acquaintances from my clubbing days fell ill and died. There were seemingly endless memorial gatherings where a group of friends would honor the memory of one of their own. I began keeping a list of the dead people I knew. Before I realized it, there were ten people, then fifteen. Ed died in June—the second close friend after Metro. I was so glad that John and I were together. We felt fairly secure about our health since we had been in a long-term, committed relationship for nearly eight years at this point.

Although the vast majority of Americans with AIDS were men who had sex with other men, that simple fact seemed to be glossed over by the media coverage and tepid political response, as though it were something embarrassing to be shoved under the rug. Within the gay community, there was a feeling of abandonment. There still were no real treatments. If you had AIDS you were a dead man walking. We felt profound sorrow, and also increasing anger.

✳✳✳

We moved into our weekend house in 1986 just in time for the holidays. There wasn't much there yet except for a mattress and a stereo and a Christmas tree. We had our annual Christmas dinner with Gail and Michael and Doug in the country. The next few months were spent outfitting the house—painting, buying furniture, setting up a studio space so that I could work both in New York and in the North Fork. We fenced in the yard so that Maggie could have the run of it all.

Early in 1987 San Francisco AIDS activist Cleve Jones made a large quilt panel in memory of his friend Marvin Feldman. Jones and a group of friends were searching for a way to honor the memory of the AIDS dead. The idea of an enormous collective quilt was inspired by a spontaneous demonstration of solidarity at a candlelight march in 1985, when a city wall was covered with pieces of paper, each with the name of a person who had died of AIDS. Jones and his friends took the idea and started an organization called the NAMES Project. They put the word out in the gay community nationwide and the panels came flooding in. Each quilt panel had to be three feet by six feet, the approximate shape and size of a grave. Each was a handmade expression of sorrow in memory of a specific person who died of AIDS. Several of Ed Krisher's friends chipped in to have a panel made in his memory.

While the AIDS quilt was a loving memorial as well as a pointed reminder of lives lost, the gay community grew increasingly angry at the lack of response to the carnage. The AIDS Coalition to Unleash Power (ACT UP) was a grassroots movement organized in March 1987 by AIDS activists who were fed up with playing nice with a nonresponsive political and corporate medical system. Larry Kramer, who was among other things a screenwriter and playwright, became an unofficial spokesperson for ACT UP. Mr. Kramer had been one of the founders of GMHC, but he had been forced out because of his uncompromising views and abrasive personal style. In the beginning Mr. Kramer had been like a prophet in the wilderness with his ideas about personal responsibility. He insisted that promiscuity increased the likelihood of transmission and thus was the reason gay men were dying, and according to him, it followed that we had to change that way of living. In 1985, a new play by Mr. Kramer was produced in New York. *The Normal Heart* was a powerful drama about the early years of the epidemic, based upon his personal experiences as an activist. It was the one of the first major works of art specifically about AIDS.

ACT UP called itself "a diverse, non-partisan group of individuals, united in *anger* and committed to direct action to end the AIDS crisis." Besides gay men, ACT UP drew the support of lesbians, people of color, and many heterosexuals. The strategy of direct action meant disrupting official events with chanting and taunting to create an unruly physical presence. A favorite tactic was the "die-in." Protestors would simply lie down in the street or on the floor and play dead. They had to be physically carried away. The message of anger was directed at institutional homophobia, which from the beginning had hampered the response to the epidemic, as well as anger at corporate greed, with obscene price-gouging of drugs by pharmaceutical companies. Anger also focused on government

An ACT UP protester on the streets of New York City, 1989.

inaction because gay people were not considered an important constituency and most conservative politicians were homophobic. ACT UP's motto, Silence = Death, was literally true. ACT UP activists were an important voice as the crisis wore on, and their in-your-face tactics produced some solid results by keeping AIDS in the news. One of ACT UP's greatest accomplishments was pushing government agencies and drug companies to accelerate testing of medications and lower the costs of existing drugs. ACT UP also provided an important psychological boost for the gay community, which had been badly battered by grief and despair. After six years of living with the horror of AIDS in our midst, taking collective action was incredibly empowering.

During the summer of 1987, we settled into a routine that would continue for a few years. John had his nine-to-five job, and with two studio setups I could work either in the city or in the country. I normally spent two or three days midweek in the city and then drove out with Maggie for long weekends. I could do the shopping and get things ready for Friday evenings, when John would take the train out. By now we were pretty well outfitted and enjoyed having friends out for weekends. Joe Palmeri, who had become John's

ACT UP poster by artist Keith Haring, 1989.

best friend in New York, had a standing invitation. He spent many weekends with us and often brought along a date. Recently retired, Joe had a flexible schedule and became our go-to dog-sitter when we wanted to travel. There was one more addition to our group of friends. After Metro's death Doug had started seeing a nice young man named Marc Beckerman, who worked in the theater as assistant to a Broadway director. Marc was a gentle soul, quiet and soft-spoken. I was so happy that Doug had a new companion. Eventually Marc moved in with Doug and became office manager for Doug's business as well. We often hung out on weekends.

***

In June 1987 a monumental piece of investigative reporting was published. *And the Band Played On: Politics, People, and the AIDS Epidemic* by Randy Shilts is a searing and devastating indictment of the political, medical, and media establishments and their mishandling of the epidemic. The title was taken from the name of a popular song from the 1890s and also recalled the groundbreaking play from 1968—*The Boys in the Band*. In the more than 630 pages of meticulously researched and almost granular detail, Mr. Shilts's book placed the early years of the AIDS epidemic, particularly in San Francisco, under the microscope. The book ends with the death of Rock Hudson in 1985. In recent years, some of Mr. Shilts's facts and opinions have been questioned, but it must be remembered that his book was written as though from the front lines of a war zone as the bombs were falling. Mr. Shilts himself also became infected with HIV and died in 1994. In spite of its flaws, the book is still a monumental achievement, as it was the first, and for a long time the only, comprehensive account of what was happening. For gay people, it is still an infuriating read.

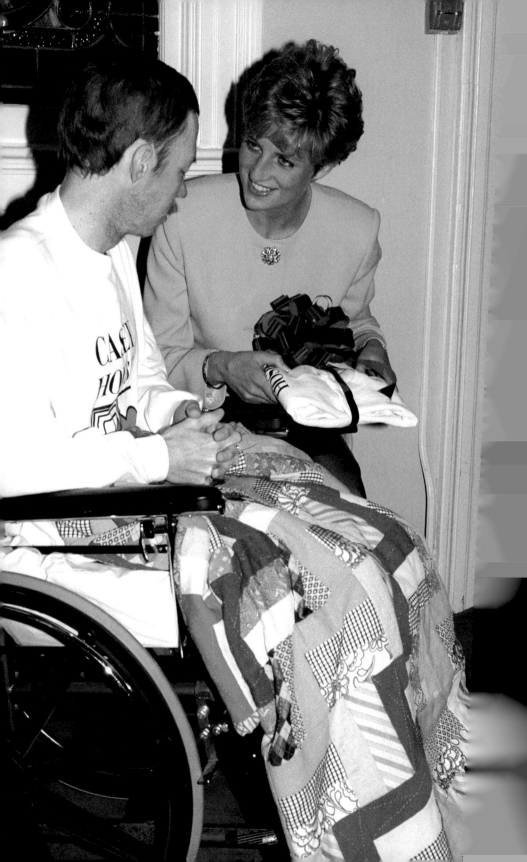

March 1987

After fast-tracking the process, the FDA approved the first antiretroviral drug, called AZT, a faint glimmer of hope for an eventual effective treatment. They also issued regulations expanding access to promising new medications. AZT was not a cure for AIDS, but for some it appeared to slow the progress of HIV, although it came with serious side effects, such as headaches, nausea, vomiting, insomnia, fatigue, muscle pain, and loss of appetite.

April 19, 1987

Princess Diana of England made international headlines by closely interacting with AIDS patients in the hospital without wearing gloves. She went on to become a passionate advocate for people living with HIV, opening the way for other celebrities to become involved.

April 29, 1987

A second type of blood test for HIV was approved. Called the Western blot test, it was far more accurate than the original test from 1985. By now safeguards were in place for confidentiality, and so this time, after two more years of living with constant fear and uncertainty, many gay men went to be tested, and doctors used the test to determine a diagnosis.

May 31, 1987

President Ronald Reagan finally made his first public policy speech about AIDS and established a presidential commission on HIV. The crisis had become impossible for him to ignore any longer. The first deaths had been more than six long years before.

Princess Diana receives a gift from an AIDS patient,
Toronto, Canada, 1991.

As the summer wound down, and autumn was in the air, we had a visitor from California. Hal Wilson was one of our very best LA friends. John had known him for many years. Hal was a successful real estate agent. We spent a few days in New York, a few days on the North Fork, and then we went to Washington, DC, to see the AIDS Memorial Quilt. Ed Krisher had also been a good friend of Hal's. He was part of the group that had a panel made for Ed only a few months before. We visited the great monuments, the Vietnam War Memorial, the Capitol, and the presidential memorials. Hal had never been to DC, and it was fun showing him the sights. But it was the AIDS quilt that made the most powerful impact.

The quilt was displayed on the National Mall beginning on October 11, 1987, as part of the National March on Washington for Lesbian and Gay Rights. It was a brilliant crisp October day, with an intense blue sky and some hazy white clouds. Part of the lawn of the National Mall, an area the size of a football field, was covered with all 1,920 quilt panels that had been made so far. The individual panels were arranged in separate segments of eight panels each so that they could be displayed with some space around each segment for walking paths. It took some searching, but we found Ed's panel. By chance, it was included in a segment that incorporated one of several Rock Hudson panels. More than half a million people went to see the quilt that weekend. The energy between the brilliant blue sky and the colorful quilt panels was electric, while the atmosphere was somber and hushed. Each panel was a personal tribute to someone who had died from the people who loved them.

During the trip, Hal revealed that he had been tested for HIV and that he was positive. He had no symptoms yet, but his doctor had him on a regimen of AZT. We knew several people who had been tested by now. Those who were positive lived with a grim knowledge of what lay in store for them. Those who were negative were relieved but conflicted. Why them, and not others? It seemed like life or death was determined merely by an arbitrary throw of the dice. A casual sexual encounter many years before that you might not even remember could kill you, or many casual encounters that you had over the years might not. And even if you were in a committed monogamous relationship, your partner's past encounters could affect you as well. Before Thanksgiving, John and I finally made the decision to be tested. After years of apprehension and fear, we wanted to ease our minds. It was excruciating to wait for the confidential test results that would determine our fate. We went to the doctor together. First I went in and got my result: negative. Then it was John's turn. His test was positive.

John was infected with HIV. The doctor started him immediately on a regimen of AZT. We were thunderstruck. It was not what we had expected.

10.
The Bucket List

At first there were tears and some sleepless nights. John had no symptoms. He seemed as healthy as ever, but he had a bad reaction to the AZT. It made him nauseous and fluish, so his dosage was adjusted so that it was tolerable, and gradually the side effects eased up. Right after New Year's he had some good news. His boss, the chief financial officer of the magazine company, was retiring, and John was offered the job. A big promotion and more money raised our spirits, and we decided to finally do some things we had talked about but postponed. Today it's called a bucket list: things you want to make sure you do before you die. We did our best to put the threat of AIDS on a back burner and to plow right ahead with life. Without symptoms it was easy to live in denial.

In April 1988, Hal Wilson joined John and me for a trip to London and Paris. He was easygoing, fun, and funny, so he was a perfect travel companion. It was a wonderful trip. I had been to London and Paris alone in 1970 as a backpacking grad student, but John and Hal were newbies. We did London first, hitting all the tourist spots. Then we rented a car and drove to Dover, where we took the hovercraft to Calais, and from there the train to Paris. My

John in Venice, Italy, October 1992.

favorite moment of the entire trip was our taxi ride from the Gare du Nord train station to our hotel near the Arc de Triomphe. It was twilight, just as the city lights were coming up. It was so beautiful. John was gawking at the unexpectedly vast, magnificent scale of Paris, and as he gripped my hand I saw a tear trickle down his cheek. During the trip we paid a visit to the Paris Flea Market, where I bought a large antique tapestry. We managed to smuggle it back home folded up in the bottom of a suit bag without paying the duty, and it hung in our home for many years as a souvenir of that trip.

Since John was still healthy, his HIV-positive status sort of receded into the background. We didn't forget about it, but it was our new normal. After a while it didn't seem to affect our daily lives. John had his job. I was exhibiting paintings annually in group or solo shows. We had the routine of city/country living. We got into the habit of an annual trip to California to see our friends. Richard Gillmore, our Hollywood friend, had moved to Palm Springs, a desert resort community, after losing a boyfriend to AIDS. So we always spent time there as well as in Los Angeles.

Right after New Year's in 1989, we lost Maggie. One day she just couldn't get up, so we drove her out to our vet in the country and reluctantly put her down. We had no choice. She was almost eleven years old, which is positively ancient for a Great Dane. Because I worked from home, she was my constant companion, and I missed her terribly. John and I waited a while in our grief, but we both wanted another dog. After doing some research we went to upstate New York to get another Great Dane puppy. This one was a black beauty with a small white blaze on her chest. We called her Willie. When we took her home at eight weeks old, she already weighed twenty pounds.

✳ ✳ ✳

Late that spring we went on a cruise to Bermuda as part of the bucket-list tour. Neither of us had ever been on a big ship at sea, so it was fun as well as very interesting. Bermuda was lovely. The ship was our hotel. We went sightseeing, biking around the island, and snorkeling. One week was exactly the right amount of time to live on a boat. But the best thing I remember about that cruise was the stirring experience of sailing out of New York Harbor at dusk and returning a week later at dawn with the magnificent backdrop of the Statue of Liberty, Ellis Island, and the glittering towers of Lower Manhattan.

My list of dead friends and acquaintances was up to about twenty. More of our good friends began having symptoms of HIV infection. Hal's health declined after our trip, and now he was in and out of the hospital. When Frank Cioffi found out he was ill, he retired on disability, and after a while was finally forced to move back to Brooklyn into his aging parents' home so that they could care for him as his illness progressed. Joe Bonanno and I went together to Brooklyn to visit him a few times, but Frank was in increasingly bad shape. It was so sad to see. He had always been such a vibrant, optimistic man. Tim Bennett gave us the bad news that Bill Hunter had been having some of the early symptoms for a while. Two of my Pines housemates became ill. Both of them fell into a deep depression. Carl Johnson began drinking heavily as his health slowly declined. Roger Blackmon, who was always very reserved to begin with, began keeping to himself more and more, to the point of being reclusive. AIDS is death in slow motion, and after years of good luck, now it was all around us.

But the bucket list continued, and in early May 1990, we spent eight days white-water rafting down the Colorado River through Grand Canyon. It was not kayaking or anything requiring knowledge or skill, but more a kind of dude ranch rafting adventure. But it was no less exciting for that. The vessels were big Korean War–era rubber pontoon boats. Our expedition had two boats in tandem. Each boat could hold up to fifteen people with a crew of two. Each boat also held an enormous ice chest full of food. Late every afternoon, after a day on the river, the crew beached the boats, set up a propane kitchen right on the edge of the Colorado, and cooked a feast while we set up our tents. Dinner was different every evening: fried trout, grilled steaks, roasted chicken, pizza. One night we even had Mexican food with margaritas. The crew made a hearty breakfast every morning at dawn before heading out for another day on the river. In the early morning chill, running rapids and getting soaked, we took nips of brandy to help keep warm. Our only responsibilities were to help load and unload the boat every day, to pitch our own tent, and to store our gear properly in a waterproof duffle bag provided by the rafting company. Otherwise we just hung on for dear life and enjoyed the ride, marveled at the scenery, and sometimes got very wet.

From the very first minute on the river, we were swept up in an ever-changing landscape that became more and more magnificent as we entered the depths of Grand Canyon. Running scores of rapids was absolutely thrilling. For the entire adventure we were compelled to live in the moment, because the moment was so extraordinary, so outside of our normal existence, that the real world of our daily lives was completely forgotten. It was one of the greatest experiences of my life. At the end, we were helicoptered out of the canyon to a ranch on the South Rim, where we showered and cleaned up after a week in the wilderness. Then we took a short flight in a Cessna to Las Vegas. Within a few hours we went from the serene grandeur of Grand Canyon to crowds of people, flashing lights, and clanging slot machines. Talk about whiplash!

John in the depths of Grand Canyon, Arizona, May 1990.

After a couple of days in Vegas, we went to LA to see our friends there. John and I visited Hal Wilson in the hospital. We were joined by Richard Gillmore, who drove in from Palm Springs. It was a shock to see how much weight Hal had lost. He had been tall and lanky. Now he seemed shrunken and scrawny. He had always been proud of his thick red hair, but now it was thin and dull. There were several small purple Kaposi's sarcoma lesions visible on his neck and arms. One of us went to the hospital cafeteria and brought back some sandwiches. We sat around in the hospital room eating, joking, and wisecracking, just as we always did. Hal had seemed despondent when we arrived. He perked up as we talked, although he didn't eat much. Something really funny made him nearly choke with laughter. You could see that laughing really hurt, but he dismissed the pain saying, "At least I'm laughing today." There were tears when we left. We were back in the real world. It was the last time we saw Hal.

By the early 1990s, as the epidemic peaked in America, a number of famous people had either died with AIDS, or announced that they were infected. Everyone was shocked when basketball phenomenon Magic Johnson made his announcement. Greg Louganis, Olympic diving champion, also went public with his diagnosis. Among the celebrities who died were fashion designer Perry Ellis, disco singer Sylvester, tennis champion Arthur Ashe, TV actress Amanda Blake, TV pianist Liberace, artist Keith Haring, photographer Robert Mapplethorpe, Broadway director/choreographer Michael Bennett, rock star Freddie Mercury, ballet star Rudolf Nureyev, movie star Anthony Perkins, and science fiction author Isaac Asimov. As the casualties mounted, the deaths of famous people helped to defuse the terrible stigma associated with AIDS.

Ryan White had gone on to live with AIDS five years longer than his doctors predicted. He died on April 8, 1990, one month before his high school graduation. He was eighteen years old. Today the Health Resources and Services Administration's Ryan White HIV/AIDS Program provides a comprehensive system of HIV primary medical care, essential support services, and medications for low-income people living with HIV who are uninsured and underserved.

Later, in 1992, openly gay rock star Sir Elton John was inspired by Ryan White's life and death to establish a nonprofit organization to help fund frontline partners to prevent infections, fight stigma, and provide treatment with love, compassion, and dignity for the most vulnerable groups affected by HIV around the world. (As of September 2020 the Elton John AIDS Foundation had raised nearly half a billion dollars for the cause.)

But certain conservatives only doubled down on their irrational homophobia. Rush Limbaugh, a right-wing talk-radio personality with a huge audience, used his platform to gay-bash dead men. In 1990 he had a regular segment during which he would harangue about "godless gays" getting what they deserved and play songs like "Back in the Saddle," "Kiss Him Goodbye," and "Looking for Love in All the Wrong Places." He even would read off the names of people who had died and then ring bells and whistles in a macabre and revolting celebration of their deaths.

✳ ✳ ✳

The North Fork has a thriving wine industry of small vineyards. That summer one of them, Pindar Vineyards, hired me to paint a series of wine labels, so that was my very pleasant job for a few months. I was constantly busy with new paintings, and it was my practice to always have something up on the easel. Work was good, I recall, but otherwise, my memories become murky. For the next few years the bad news was relentless, and it all sort of blurs together. Different people were sick at the same time. Their illnesses overlapped. Friends died, but now I'm not sure exactly when, or in what order. There was an emotionally exhausting and soul-numbing dull sorrow that never ended, punctuated by sharp pain when a friend died a terrible death. In the meantime life all around us carried on, as if oblivious to the carnage, and we carried on as well. We had no choice.

Hal Wilson passed away in Los Angeles. His friends held a memorial, but we could not attend. Frank Cioffi died in Brooklyn. Joe Bonanno and I went to the funeral. In the taxi back to Manhattan we reminisced about our disco days, now nearly fifteen years in the past. Carl Johnson died in the hospital—whether technically from AIDS or alcohol abuse, it doesn't really matter. And Roger Blackmon died by suicide. Always very reserved and private, now that he was ill, Roger spent most of his time in his bedroom. Since he had his own bathroom, it wasn't unusual for him to withdraw for a day. Robert understood and respected Roger's privacy. But this time, after nearly two days of noncommunication, Robert became alarmed. He was shocked to find Roger in his bed, dead from an overdose, with a note that said he just could not face the ordeal of dying from AIDS. Robert was shattered. Overcome with grief and guilt, he felt that by leaving Roger alone, he had left his best friend to die.

It simply would not end. The horror of it all was relentless and overwhelming. Doug's second partner, Marc Beckerman, began exhibiting symptoms. And then, at some point Robert told us that he had tested positive for HIV and was beginning to feel ill. He had known for a while, but had kept it to himself until now. I was devastated by this news. Robert was one of the closest friends of my life. And to top it off, John's health now began to decline. At first it was just a lack of energy, a period of sweaty nights, some weight loss—nothing dramatic. But we both knew it was just the beginning of a long and terrible ordeal with only one possible outcome. When my list of the dead reached number forty-one, I stopped keeping count. It seemed pointless.

Over that winter Robert became very sick. The purple lesions of Kaposi's sarcoma appeared on his feet and legs. He lost a lot of weight. Always burly, now he was thin and gaunt. Over time the lesions on one of his feet turned gangrenous. His foot had to be amputated above the ankle. After the surgery he declined rapidly. His boyfriend, David, moved into Roger's empty room to care for him. With his suppressed immune system, his leg never really healed. Carl's death, followed closely by Roger's tragic suicide, had taken a terrible emotional toll. Robert could get around with crutches at home in his apartment, but he needed a wheelchair for outside. We spent some evenings keeping him and David company in front of the TV. John and I took them out to a quiet dinner near their apartment a couple of times. We took turns pushing his wheelchair. Going out was very difficult for Robert, both physically and psychologically. The Village is a small neighborhood, and he wanted to avoid seeing any casual acquaintances in his condition. It was heartbreaking.

John's illness was beginning to take more of a toll. He was experiencing bouts of extreme fatigue, and it was time to make some decisions. He wanted to retire before it was forced upon him, and so he informed his employer of his condition and negotiated a retirement schedule and severance package. Early in 1992 we put the New York loft on the market and sold it a couple of months before his retirement began. In late summer John formally retired, and we moved into the North Fork house full-time. After nearly twenty-five years in Philadelphia, New York, or Los Angeles, it was beyond strange to no longer call a big city home.

There would be one last bucket-list adventure. We spent the month of October 1992 in Italy. First a week in Rome, then another in Florence, and finally a week in Venice. We spent a few days between each city traveling around the Italian countryside in a rental car, with side day trips to Pisa, Siena, Padua, Bologna, and Ravenna. It was a dream come true for me, since Italian painting was one of my major interests in art history grad school, and John had to put up with a lot of visits to museums and churches to see paintings. We had been fairly frugal up until then, but for the week in Venice we splurged on a deluxe old-guard hotel, the Bauer-Gruenwald. We had two luxurious rooms with a balcony overlooking the entrance to the Grand Canal, close to the Piazza San Marco, the ceremonial center of the city. While we were there, Venice experienced one of its periodic floods. For a couple of days the piazza was under about eighteen inches of water. Our hotel lobby was flooded. The staff piled up the furniture, rolled up the oriental rugs and put them on top. It was a well-established routine for them. We got black trash bags and duct tape and fashioned makeshift "boots" rather than buying some. It all was part of the adventure.

When we started our trip we knew that Robert was in very grave condition. We left our travel information with David, and about a week before the end of our vacation, he called with the news that Robert had taken a sudden turn and was in the ICU. He lapsed into a coma and died the day before we flew back to New York. Robert's death was the bitter climax of a long period of dealing with never-ending sickness and death. He was my closest friend of all of those who had died, and I loved him like a brother. But so many people I knew had succumbed to AIDS in a relatively short time that by the time Robert died, it barely registered. After so much sorrow, I had apparently developed a thick skin for self-protection. There was merely a kind of numb acceptance. I felt guilty that we had not been there for his last days. We didn't get to say goodbye. It seemed unreal then, and it still does to this day.

John and me in Rome, Italy, October 1992.

11.
Home Alone

It was strange having John around full-time. For twenty years I had been alone every weekday with my work. Painting was my job. In the country I had been painting in a living room alcove, but now I set up a proper studio in a large storage room above our garage so that I could actually leave the house to go to work and be alone. I needed the solitude. I didn't know it yet, but I was about to embark upon a second career.

A couple of years before, I had been offered the opportunity to illustrate a picture book for children. When it was proposed to me, I jumped at the chance. After twenty years as a gallery artist, I was ready to shake things up a bit. My gallery paintings were always quite large. Each typically took weeks to do. For book illustrations I had to teach myself to work at a much smaller scale and far more rapidly. But I had always made paintings in series, with a common theme, meant to be exhibited together, so it was a fairly natural transition. Early in 1993 my first book as an illustrator, *Horses with Wings,* by Dennis Haseley, was published to excellent reviews. And then, almost immediately, I got a contract for a second book. I had enjoyed the bookmaking process and was eager for more. It was

John's illness begins to show, late 1993.

a completely different collaborative creative experience than that of a solitary gallery painter. And the idea that my work would be out there in the hands of thousands of kids was so very exciting. This time my editor encouraged me to try my hand at writing as well as illustrating. In 1975 I had exhibited a series of paintings called *Zeppelin Variations*. I had done a ton of research then, so I decided to write about balloons and airships. I wrote on a primitive laptop—nothing more than a word processor. I worked on the book intermittently for the next two years, first writing and then painting, as events unfolded.

John spent his time puttering around the house, reading, watching TV, listening to music—a bit at loose ends after twenty years in the corporate world. He took on the project of organizing the hundreds of photos he had taken over the years into a series of photo albums. In the autumn of 1993, we went to Palm Springs for a visit with Richard Gillmore. Tim and Bill, along with a few other LA friends, came out to the desert to see us. It was nice to see everyone, but also grim. Bill Hunter's illness was advancing, and he was gaunt and hollow-eyed. By now John had lost some weight, too. For the first time I noticed his neck was getting skinny, and he looked a bit haggard. We all had been living with AIDS for so long that it was just part of our lives. We didn't discuss it. We were a group of old friends, sharing a weekend, trying to have a good time. It would be our last good time all together.

Back in New York, the progress of Marc Beckerman's illness had been gradual, not a sudden shock like Metro's. This time Doug was prepared and was able to take charge, but Marc's illness took a turn for the worse that autumn and he died. Doug was alone again. Two partners, both dead.

***

In December 1993 a major Hollywood film with AIDS as the subject was released. In *Philadelphia*, popular actor Tom Hanks starred as a closeted gay lawyer who is fired from his job at a prestigious law firm when his bosses discover that he has AIDS. Heartthrob Denzel Washington played the attorney who takes on the job of suing Hank's employers for discrimination. Washington's character is homophobic, but as a Black man, he has also suffered from discrimination, and during the course of the movie he is moved to change his opinions by the dignity of Hanks's character in the face of injustice. *Philadelphia* was a powerful drama that was one of the first mainstream movies to deal with AIDS and homophobia. John insisted that we go to see it. We really didn't discuss it, but for me the movie was difficult to watch. Afterward I bought the soundtrack.

During the holidays John began having more serious health problems. There was a relentless fatigue, fluish symptoms, and, gradually, chronic indigestion. He had always been subject to occasional acid reflux and often popped Tums, but this was different. It didn't go away. Right after the New Year, the doctor did a biopsy. We got the devastating news that John had a moderately advanced cancer of the esophagus. We wondered that this was not a typical AIDS opportunistic disease, but the doctor explained that John's weakened immune system had potentially allowed something that was already there to grab hold. John's father had died of esophageal cancer only a few years before. Perhaps there was a genetic tendency for the cancer. In one way we were lucky, in that John had few of the other horrible infections associated with AIDS.

So it began. First, a regimen of chemotherapy. A port catheter—a device that allows intravenous fluids to be administered without puncturing the skin each time—was surgically implanted in John's chest. The chemo left John weak and listless. He spent most of his time in bed or reclining on the sofa watching TV. After he had recovered somewhat from that, he endured several rounds of radiation, leaving his esophagus burned and raw. He could drink liquids, but it was nearly impossible to swallow any solid food. He was on heavy-duty pain meds, and the port was also used for nourishment. John could have had a feeding tube implanted so that the liquid food could be injected directly into his stomach, but he had seen his dad suffer through this extremely uncomfortable process, and so he refused it. During the weeks of radiation treatments, John became so weak that he was pretty much confined to bed. He lost his hair and was totally bald for a while, and when his hair started growing back, it had turned white. He was losing weight and strength. During the several months of treatments and recovery periods, we had visitors. Doug and Gail and Michael stopped by regularly on weekends, and city friends made day trips to visit. Everyone was shocked by John's transformation in just a few months. We were happy to have the visitors, but basically it was just John and me and Willie, waiting it out.

The chemo and radiation bought us some time. The progress of the cancer was temporarily halted. But even so, John had no energy and spent most of the time in bed. Eventually he was able to swallow soft food again. Sometimes the house became claustrophobic to me. I coped by working. Most days I was up in the studio for several hours of painting. I had come up with the idea of an illustrated version of the famous short story "The Masque of the Red Death," by Edgar Allan Poe. In the story a group of revelers at a masked ball are oblivious that the figure of death is among them. What could be more timely? I came up with the idea for a series of eight or nine images to illustrate it. I put the zeppelin book aside and did two large trial paintings. Done partly to show myself that this idea could work, I knew also that the paintings might be used to sell the idea to a publisher. When Joe Palmeri saw these dark and somber paintings he asked if I was doing okay. I assured him that the work was therapeutic for me. That summer I also did a portrait of John as a surprise for his forty-sixth birthday in August. I worked from a photo taken during our Bermuda cruise, just five years before.

The news from Laguna Beach was very bad. During the late spring Bill had a bout of Pneumocystis pneumonia. His wasting syndrome was well advanced. Eventually he was so weak that he fell and fractured his hip and was in the hospital one last time. It was clear that he was dying, so he and Tim made the decision for him to come home, directly into hospice. Hospice is end-of-life care, when death is inevitable. Active treatment is ended, and pain relief becomes the goal. Hospice at home requires a family member to become the primary caregiver. As his partner, Tim took charge of Bill's care. A hospice nurse visited regularly to take vital signs and adjust pain medication, and an orderly came to help keep the patient clean and change the sheets. The decision to go into hospice at home involves an understanding and acceptance that death is imminent, and it requires a real commitment on the part of the loved one in charge. Bill lingered on for several weeks, and he finally died in mid-July. Tim called the next day with the news. Tim Bennett and Bill Hunter had been together for more than twenty years. Death was back in our lives.

Bill Hunter's face shows the ravages of AIDS, Palm Springs, California, late 1993.

12.

The End

A couple of weeks later, John began having terrible chest pains. The cancer was active again. The doctor told us that it was just a matter of time. After a while John's discomfort became intolerable, and he went into the hospital, where the pain could be treated more aggressively. I went to the hospital twice a day, and every time during the drive, both going and coming, I played the second movement of Beethoven's String Quartet no. 8—a somber, sublime adagio. John was dying. I had to suck it up and stay focused and strong. This piece of music would become for me his elegy.

During that last stay in the hospital, the doctor, God bless him, allowed me to bring Willie into John's room as a surprise. The room was at one end of a corridor by an emergency exit, and the doctor personally escorted us up the back stairs and directly into the hospital room. John was surprised and delighted, but poor Willie was confused and distracted by the smells and sounds of the hospital.

The first display of the AIDS Quilt on the National Mall, Washington, DC, October 1987.

I had kept all of our friends informed about what was happening, but I was absolutely stunned when Tim called to ask if he might fly back east to see John before it was too late. After all, Bill had died only a few weeks before. Tim stayed with me for a couple of days while John was in the hospital. I had kept his visit as a surprise, and John was overcome and shed some tears when Tim first walked into the hospital room with me. Tim shared his hospice experience with us, and he and I had some frank discussions at home in the evening. Tim's kind and loving gesture in the face of his own grief solidified an already good, close friendship into a permanent bond. From then on Tim Bennett was like a brother to me.

Things were moving quickly now. John made the decision to enter hospice. It was time to come home. I would be his primary caregiver, and it would be my responsibility and privilege to help ease him out of this world. The nurse in charge came to check out our environment in advance. They brought in a hospital bed and the equipment for administering medication intravenously through his port. John's elderly mother, Helen, flew in from California a couple of days before he came home. Technically she was his stepmother, but she was the only mother he had ever known. We had been friendly for a long time. I welcomed her help and, most importantly, John wanted her there. When he arrived at home, they set him up in the bed and hooked everything up. He was in a lot of pain, so they put him on a morphine drip. He could no longer swallow, and was hydrated by intravenous glucose. There would be no more food or drink. If his mouth was dry, we used a damp sponge on a stick, like a Popsicle, to moisten his lips. During the first couple of days, he was able to walk to the bathroom, but as he became weaker, he was fitted with a catheter. We had gotten a wheelchair so that he could leave the bedroom, but we never even used it. John was now confined to what would become his deathbed. I kept an extra dog bed for Willie in the room so that she could keep him company whenever she wanted. She was a sweet and gentle dog. She would sometimes stand beside the bed and rest her big Great Dane head right next to his arm. Dogs know.

It seems cruel and harsh, but the doctor and the hospice nurse explained that death by starvation was the best option, and that's what John chose. Prolonging things by intravenous feeding would only give the cancer more time to ravage his body and cause even more pain. The process took about two and a half weeks after he was confined to his bed. The nurse came every other day to take vitals and adjust his morphine dosage in an attempt to keep ahead of the pain, and an orderly came regularly to clean him and change his sheets. They prepared us by explaining in great detail the physical and psychological process of death, and what we might expect. To keep my sanity through the final ordeal, I fixed upon the idea of doing everything *properly* and with dignity: taking care of the house and our finances, informing all of our friends and families about what was going on, making arrangements for what would happen after his death. His mother and I had only one major conflict. Helen wanted a Catholic funeral mass for John. I knew that he wanted a simple memorial gathering for friends at home. Helen and I had words about it. Reluctantly, I forced the issue by bringing it up with John in her presence. She relented, begrudgingly, because I made it clear that it was not her decision to make.

For the first week John was fairly lucid and talkative. He asked me to play his favorite classical CDs or to put on a favorite TV show. But as he grew weaker, he spoke less and less. I gave him plenty of time alone with his mother, who would sit and watch TV with him, and we alternated nights sleeping on a foam mattress on the floor by his hospital bed. Sometimes he woke up in the middle of the night, confused, agitated, and frightened, and we wanted to be there when he did. Once when he woke up, he pointed and whispered that he saw his dad and Ed and Robert outside the window. Every few days Joe Palmeri would come out to spend the night in the room with him and give us a break. Eventually John could no longer speak. He communicated by nodding or shaking his head slightly when I asked a question. Once, he looked straight at me and silently mouthed the words, "Help me." I did not know what he meant! Help me what? Help me die? I tried to get him to continue, but there was no more. All I could do was assure him that it was okay for him to let go and stop fighting. At some point I began actively to wish for death to come and take him.

Toward the end, the morphine drip wasn't keeping up with his pain. The pump was outfitted with a button that enabled us to send an extra shot of the powerful drug into his body, but it was programmed with a strict timing schedule so that he could not overdose. It seemed so stupid. Why would that have mattered? For the last few days we pushed that button whenever the timer allowed. By now he had stopped communicating completely, but was not in a coma. He was awake and watched, aware of us and our conversations.

The end came on Friday, September 9, 1994, at 10:00 a.m. Joe had been there helping out for a couple of days. That morning was bright and sunny, so he had taken Helen out of the claustrophobic house for a drive and some lunch. The hospice orderly was there, and I was helping her change John's sheets while he remained in the bed, a standard hospital maneuver. We rolled John onto his side and I held him in place as she started the sheet-changing process. Suddenly his breath caught, and he made a funny noise. The orderly looked at me and said quietly, "The death rattle. This is it." And so it happened that I was holding him as he died. I was so glad that his mother wasn't there for this last profound moment between John and me. I truly believe that he had held on until she left us alone. I whispered in his ear that I loved him. He stopped breathing and watched me as I saw the life gradually leave his eyes. They remained open. I tried to close them like they do in the movies, but they would not stay completely closed. I brought Willie in, and I held John's hand as we sat with him while the orderly gave us privacy and made her telephone calls. The hospice nurse came immediately, spoke with our doctor on the phone, and officially pronounced him dead. Then the undertaker, whom I had arranged in advance, collected his body. I wanted to help carry him out to the hearse, but the nurse would not let me. She said it was not a good idea for my peace of mind to have a body bag as my last memory of his physical presence.

Strange, but immediately upon his death, I could no longer call up the sound of his voice in my mind. It still has never returned to me. John David Martin had turned forty-six years old exactly one month before he died. I turned forty-seven years old exactly one month after.

IN VERY SHORT ORDER, WE WATCHED AS ENTIRE COMMUNITIES VANISHED. THE THEATER CROWD. THE DESIGN CROWD. MUSICIANS. ARCHITECTS. FASHION PEOPLE. GALLERISTS. THE ART PEOPLE. STAPLE GUN QUEENS. THEY DIED IN DROVES.

THEN THERE WERE THE ORDINARY GUYS WHO WE WOULD SEE OUT AND ABOUT. THEN IT WAS OUR FRIENDS. YOU MIGHT NOT SEE SOMEONE FOR SOME TIME, THEN YOU'D RUN INTO THEM ON THE STREET, SKELETAL AND LEANING ON A CANE. OR COVERED WITH KS. YOU'D SEE MEN IN MAKE-UP TRYING TO CONCEAL THEIR LESIONS. OR SITTING IN FRONT OF A PHARMACY CRYING BECAUSE THEY COULDN'T AFFORD THEIR MEDICATION. OR THEY BECAME CELIBATE AND STOPPED SEEING PEOPLE. OR THEY DISAPPEARED. OR YOU'D VISIT THEM IN HOSPITAL WHEN THEY HAD STROKES CAUSED BY THE PENTAMIDINE AND AZT THEY WERE GIVEN. OR THEY WENT BLIND. OR DEMENTED. OR THEY KILLED THEMSELVES.

YOU COULD STAY HOME NIGHTS TO DRINK AND CRY. YOU COULD WAKE UP AND CRY. YOU COULD COLLAPSE ON THE SIDEWALK OUTSIDE THE FUNERAL CHAPEL. EVERY BRUISE AND BUMP SUGGESTED INSTANT DEATH. YOU'D THINK THAT MAYBE IT WAS SLOWING DOWN AND THEN ANOTHER DOZEN PEOPLE WOULD GET SICK AND DIE.

THE WAITERS YOU FLIRTED WITH. THE BARTENDERS YOU KISSED. THE GUYS YOU WENT HOME WITH. THE SHOPKEEPERS YOU VISITED. THE PEOPLE YOU WORKED WITH. YOUR NEIGHBORS. THE DJS YOU DANCED TO. YOUR OLD DANCING FRIENDS. YOUR CRUISING BUDDIES. YOUR FUCK BUDDIES. YOUR OLD BOYFRIENDS. YOUR HUSBANDS. ALL GONE.

—MARK KANE, FACEBOOK POST ON WORLD AIDS DAY, DECEMBER 1, 2020

13.

After

John's mother became hysterical when she and Joe returned from their lunch to find that not only had John died but his body was already gone. I felt bad for her, but the events immediately after John died were determined by the nurse and had their own momentum that was out of my control. Helen stayed for a few days to decompress. John had asked to be cremated, and when his ashes were delivered a couple of days after his death, I gave Helen some of them to scatter as she wished in California. Gail and Michael had us over for a somber dinner the night before she left. Now, full of grief, I was eager to see her go. Her presence had become awkward and irritating for me. I needed to be alone to process everything that had happened. I spent about a month in a sort of daze, bouncing off the walls with nothing to do after the intensity of John's final weeks.

Late in October my older brother, Jim, flew with my mother to New York. I picked them up at LaGuardia Airport and we drove directly out to the North Fork. Jim stayed for a couple of nights, then he went home. My brother and I had never been particularly close. When you are kids, seven years' difference in age is a chasm.

His kind gesture to bring my mom to see me meant the world to me, and we have become good friends in the years since.

My mother stayed for a week. I assured her that I was okay, that I was regularly tested, and that I was not infected with HIV. Dorothy Curlee was a soft-spoken southern lady. It was comforting having her as my guest, and it gave me a focus for a week. The North Fork is beautiful in the autumn, and showing her around on her second trip there got me out of the house. At night we sat around quietly and read.

After my mother left, winter rapidly approached. The time changed. It got dark earlier and earlier. Now it was just Willie and me. I was sad, lonely, exhausted, and angry. How could John leave me alone? I sat around and brooded. Grief is brutal.

About three months after John's death, I had a memorial gathering at home. Of course Gail and Michael and Doug were there, and our remaining New York friends and many of John's former work colleagues made the drive out from the city. Tim and Richard both flew in from California. It was a relaxed and informal event. Several people spoke about him, and then everyone sat through a playlist of some serious music, as per John's explicit instructions, including the Kyrie from Beethoven's *Missa Solemnis*, the adagio from Mozart's Clarinet Quintet, the first movement of Beethoven's Violin Concerto, the Kyrie from a mass by Palestrina, and one of Mahler's *Songs of a Wayfarer*. Real heavy-duty stuff. It was all music he particularly loved, but I knew also and was privately amused that the subtle test of people's endurance was an example of his somewhat sardonic sense of humor. Then we brought out food and drinks, and everybody quietly socialized. I put on an old mix tape of 1970s soul music that Robert had made for me when we were boyfriends. It seemed particularly fitting, since Robert had introduced John and me. It was a nice, if sedate, party. After most people left, a few of my closest friends hung out for a few hours and we reminisced. We took John's ashes and scattered them at the base of a beautiful little blue spruce I had planted in the backyard during the summer before. Then we cracked open some champagne and toasted his life. I poured an entire bottle of Veuve Clicquot, his favorite champagne, over his ashes and worked them into the ground with a spade. After sixteen years together, my life partner was now only a memory.

The holidays were difficult for me, of course. We had our traditional Christmas at Gail and Michael's, but my heart was aching. I had done no work or much of anything else since John entered the hospital for the last time. After New Year's I decided that I needed a change of scene. I had been in the house almost continuously for more than a year. Joe came out to the North Fork to stay with Willie, and I met up with Richard in San Francisco. We spent a few days on a casual unplanned road trip all the way down the gorgeous Pacific Coast Highway to Laguna Beach, where we visited Tim for a couple of days. After my trip I went back to my nearly finished zeppelin book, wrapped it all up in a few weeks of work, and got it off to the publisher. After six months of intense grieving, I needed to be back in business, but that didn't mean leaving my grief behind. A few years before, John had planted a rose garden in our backyard, which he lovingly tended. There were several rose trees, and a score of bushes and two trellises with climbing roses. During his last year the roses were neglected. Now I dug up the plants and gave them to friends who were willing to replant and care for them. I could not bear to tend them. Suddenly I was busy with work. That summer Pindar Vineyards commissioned a new series of wine labels, and then I was offered a contract for my third book. It felt good to be back in a regular, normal world after more than two years in the wilderness. Willie was always by my side, and I gradually got used to being alone.

Although we could not legally marry, John and I considered ourselves to be the exact equivalent of a married couple. We had carefully made binding legal arrangements so that there could be no question about matters of inheritance. We saw what had happened to other gay men who were not prepared when relatives swooped in and took over after a partner's death. John had honored his family with a modest bequest to his niece and nephew, who were very small children. But then about six months after his death, when I thought everything was settled, Helen began sending me angry letters with wild accusations that I must have forged documents and manipulated matters for my own benefit. Then she hired a lawyer to contest our arrangements. I was first astonished, then aghast, and finally mad as hell. She had accepted and welcomed me as John's partner for sixteen years. If we had been legally married, there would simply have been no question about inheritance. There was some back-and-forth between our attorneys. After reviewing all of our documents, her lawyer finally conceded that not only were her accusations pointless, they were, in fact, potentially libelous, and that was the end of the ugly episode. I had always liked Helen, and we had what I had considered a very cordial relationship. Now that was over. I know that she was grieving, too, but that was no excuse for insulting and alienating me, and I was through with her.

***

There was one more AIDS death to endure and friend to mourn. A couple of years after John died, Joe Palmeri moved from Queens to Palm Springs, California. He had an instant social life since Richard was already in Palm Springs and Tim was in Laguna, not too far away. I revived the annual trip to California to see them all. By now Joe had been HIV-positive for a long time. He was on the HAART drug cocktail, but he had already developed serious liver problems. The new treatment proved too late for him. After only two years in California, he died suddenly of AIDS-related liver failure. Tim brought his ashes back east, and a group of us honored Joe's request to scatter them among the dunes in Fire Island Pines, the gay paradise of my young manhood, twenty long years before.

Richard Gillmore, me, and Joe Palmeri, Palm Springs, California, 1997.

After the tepid response of Republican presidents Reagan and George H. W. Bush to the AIDS epidemic, President Bill Clinton, under pressure from Democratic AIDS activists, finally issued an executive order on June 4, 1995, establishing the Presidential Advisory Council on HIV/AIDS. At last the government of the United States was stepping up to the plate with a coordinated response to the crisis.

Finally in June 1995, there was a long-sought-after breakthrough—a highly active antiviral therapy (HAART) was approved. It treated HIV infection with a combination of three or more drugs that prevented the virus from making copies of itself in the body, reducing the damage caused by HIV to the immune system and slowing down the development of AIDS. It also helped prevent transmission of the virus from one person to another. HAART was not a cure, but fifteen long years after the first AIDS deaths in the United States, there finally was an effective treatment. AIDS could now be managed in a long-term way, much like diabetes. If the disease was too far advanced, the new therapy did little good, but it literally saved the lives of thousands of people for whom the timing was right. And for new infections, it made all the difference. Most of those people never even got sick as long as they continued with HAART. Within two years the death rate in the United States from AIDS plummeted by nearly 50 percent, primarily among those gay men who had access to comprehensive health care, insurance, and medical information. It came too late for John, but today there are many older guys who were on the brink of full-blown AIDS who have gone on to lead normal, healthy lives with HAART therapy. It seems bitterly ironic that they are again at high risk in the COVID-19 pandemic.

Although the worst was finally over in the gay male community, the epidemic was not done in America. During the late 1990s, AIDS still raged in African American and Latino communities, with poverty, inferior medical care, and cultural attitudes about sex between men as factors. By 1998, the mortality rate for African Americans with AIDS was ten times that of white people, and three times that of Hispanic people. Statistically, the percentage of women with AIDS increased as well. President Clinton announced a package of initiatives specifically aimed at reducing the impact of HIV on racial and ethnic minorities. At last AIDS was being treated more as a public health issue than a political one.

As of the turn of the millennium on December 31, 2000, 774,467 people had been diagnosed with AIDS in the United States since the beginning of the epidemic; 448,060 of these were dead. The great majority of them were gay men.

The antiviral therapy (HAART) introduced in 1995 changed everything. For fifteen years a diagnosis of AIDS had come with a crushing psychological burden: the certain knowledge of the gruesome, painful death in slow motion that awaited you. Now, at a stroke, infection with HIV would no longer be an automatic death sentence.

In 1996, the AIDS Memorial Quilt was exhibited again in Washington, DC. This time, thirty-nine thousand panels covered the vast area of the National Mall, representing thirty-nine thousand lives cut tragically short.

One of two paintings inspired by Edgar Allan Poe's "The Masque of the Red Death."
I painted both during the final stages of John Martin's illness in the summer of 1994.

Me and John at Fire Island Pines,
New York, July 4th week, 1978.

Tributes.

The "Red Death" had long devastated the country.
No pestilence had ever been so fatal, or so hideous.
—Edgar Allan Poe, "The Masque of the Red Death"

Metro Crawford

died age 35

Metro was an architect, amateur gymnast, opera lover, and master of clever but really terrible puns. Doug first met Metro during our grad-school days at Penn, when Metro was a pre-med undergraduate. Metro switched to architecture, and much to my surprise, a few years later the two joined forces as partners in both life and business after Metro moved to New York. I always loved the fact that he had a set of gymnast's rings installed in their loft. According to Doug, "Metro was strong willed. It reminds me of the joke, 'Often wrong, but never in doubt,' but with Metro it was 'Often right, but still never in doubt.'"

Ed was a Midwesterner who had moved to California with John Martin in his late teens, when John was in his early twenties. Since John and Ed had been partners, we were a bit awkward with one another when I first moved to LA, but gradually, since he was still a part of John's life, we became close friends. Ed was a big strapping guy who had once been a skinny kid. He transformed himself by working out. Like John, he became an accountant, but his true love was the outdoors. He was the ringleader for camping trips with groups of friends in the wilderness north of Los Angeles. He took us to a place far from civilization called Big Meadow. It was a long way from Manhattan.

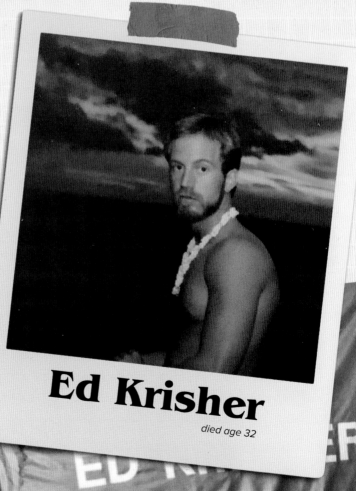

Ed Krisher

died age 32

Marc Beckerman

died age 34

Doug Peix first met Marc at a party about six months before Metro died. Marc had recently lost his own partner. In Doug's own words, "We actually connected very quickly following Metro's death. I called him to talk about the deaths of both our partners. Our mutual attraction was strong, and we shared a fatal feeling that we were likely to be next. We linked up to care for each other. Marc was very spiritual and ascribed power to crystals. He was a sweet, kind man."

Carl was a great mix of home-boy genuine and sophisticated New York cool. Plus he was hysterically funny. We shared a bedroom in Fire Island Pines during the fateful summer of 1978 when I met John. After John and I had moved back to New York from LA, the two of them became quite close, often hanging out together when I wasn't in the city. When we moved into our North Fork home, Carl's housewarming gift was a folk-art sculpture of a pelican, made from a shovel blade, a couple of big washers, and some scrap metal.

Carl Johnson

died age 42

Roger Blackmon

died age 45

Roger was Robert Cromwell's best friend. They had known one another for years before they both moved to New York and shared an apartment. Roger was a quiet, serious, introverted man. He had served in Vietnam and must have experienced terrible things. When asked about it, he would never discuss it. He worked in an office, but he spent most of his spare time mixing tracks on his dual turntables and making cassette tapes. Roger always provided the soundtrack whenever we gathered at their apartment, and we always had the best music in town.

Harold Wilson hated his name. When he was younger he tried out "Joe," but he eventually settled on Hal. A very successful real estate agent, he had grown up in Beverly Hills, and his parents worked in the movie industry. Several movie stars were family friends. Hal had bright red hair, and he could be very grand, but with his tongue firmly planted in his cheek. Besides, we knew how to take him down a notch. He had a springer spaniel named Fergie, after the Duchess of York, naturally.

Hal Wilson

died age 45

Joe Palmeri

died age 52

Joe had a strong opinion about almost everything, and he was always ready to share it with anyone who would listen. This never failed to amuse us. He hung out with John and me a lot and was perhaps John's closest friend in New York. Late in his life, after the deaths of so many friends, he was able to fulfill a lifelong dream and move to California. He had a couple of happy years there. Joe's final illness and death from AIDS a few years after starting therapy with the lifesaving drugs was a terrible shock to both his friends and family. We had all thought he would be one of the lucky ones.

Frank had a tattoo. Big deal, right? Unlike today, though, tattoos were pretty rare back then, and they weren't considered fashionable. But Frank had served in the US Navy, and his tattoo was the Navy emblem. The tattoo was beautifully done, and since Frank was well-built, it looked great on him. Frank grew up in Brooklyn and worked and lived there during the disco years. He made the big move to Manhattan in 1983, a couple of years after his summer with us in Los Angeles. It was great having him nearby, and I spent a lot of time with him. Besides being a lot of fun, Frank was very intelligent, and we had many deep and meaningful conversations over the years.

Frank Cioffi

died age 48

Bill Hunter
died age 44

Bill grew up in Hollywood. He was a quintessential California guy—big, blond, and relaxed. He and Tim lived high up in the Laguna Hills in a modern house with huge windows and a spectacular panoramic view of the Pacific Ocean and the town far below. Whenever they stayed with us in New York, which was often, Bill would always arrive with a huge armful of beautiful cut flowers. Tim was frugal; in fact it was a running joke among his friends. But Bill was not, and flowers were one of his extravagances.

Robert and I loved to dance together. Our bodies were always in contact. When we were really in the groove, sometimes people would actually stop dancing to watch us. Once at a party, someone asked why I didn't make erotic paintings. It was true that on an overt level I didn't, but Robert just looked at him and said, "Man, don't you have eyes?" It was the best compliment about my work I ever had. A few months after we met, I had a gallery show that coincided with my birthday. Below is the gift he gave me—a bolo tie with the Mona Lisa in a horseshoe—a great piece of kitsch—worthless, yet priceless to me. I used to wear it for every gallery opening.

Robert Cromwell

died age 50

John Martin

died age 46

This photograph was taken during Thanksgiving weekend 1978, when I made my secret trip to Los Angeles a few months after John and I had met. It was during this trip that we decided to join our lives together. That fateful decision was the best one I have ever made. He changed my life for the better. Of course like any couple we bickered about little things, but we were remarkably in tune with one another about the truly important things in life. Everyone who knew John was struck by his intelligence and his big, warm heart. He was my companion, my best friend, my helpmate, and my soul mate for sixteen remarkable years. This is one of my favorite photographs of him.

*Portrait of John Martin, painted as a birthday
surprise during his final summer, 1994.*

He had come like a thief in the night. And one by one dropped the revellers. . . . And Darkness and Decay and the Red Death held illimitable dominion over all.

—Edgar Allan Poe, "The Masque of the Red Death"

Epilogue.
"Being Alive, Being Alive"

Why did I never become infected with HIV? In the years before I met John, I had only two real boyfriends, Doug Capasso and Robert Cromwell. I loved them both, but we did not take the step of becoming life partners. Otherwise I was footloose and basically unattached for much of my twenties. I ran with a very fast crowd in New York at the very moment when thousands of young men were unknowingly becoming infected, and I certainly must have been exposed to HIV. Eventually I entered into a committed relationship, and then my partner got sick and died, but I did not. The same is true for Doug Peix, Richard Gillmore, Tim Bennett, and several other people I know. It is clear that certain sexual activities are riskier than others, and some people are more careful in their sex lives than others. But there may have been another factor. In 2005 a study was published which speculated that about ten percent of people of European descent have a natural immunity to HIV, inherited from the survivors of the great plagues of the Middle Ages. Although unproven and controversial, it is an absolutely fascinating and important theory that does nothing to change the disturbing fact that while so many died, I did not. Genetics? Fate? Pure chance? A throw of the dice? Whichever it was, I was lucky.

My painting of the ebony clock from Edgar Allan Poe's famous story.

More than a quarter of a century has passed since John died. After being alone for almost exactly two years, I met someone: a British bloke named Nicholas Atkins. We started hanging out, and after a few years as casual boyfriends, we eventually joined forces as life partners. We are still together. There have been more Great Danes. After Willie there was Lola, then Jacky, who was joined by Garbo, and then Monaco. Three at once—a house full of giant dogs. After the second book, I did a third, and then a fourth. To my own surprise I had become an author as well as a painter. Gradually this second career making children's books became the main event. Now I have published fifteen books. After personal tragedy ended one phase of my life, I made a new start. The AIDS horror was perhaps the central trauma of my life, but I survived and had the privilege of growing old. Hundreds of thousands of others in the United States did not.

* * *

The AIDS Quilt was displayed once more in Washington, DC, during July 2012. This time there were nearly fifty thousand panels, and volunteers had to swap them in and out in order to give each one a chance to be displayed. What began as a memorial for one man has become a memorial for thousands. The AIDS Quilt is an important cultural touchstone and a magnificent and very moving masterpiece of folk art with an important place in American history.

Even though the acute crisis of the 1980s and 1990s in America has passed, AIDS still simmers in the United States. HIV thrives on apathy and ignorance. Many young people today regard AIDS as ancient history, and, as young people often do, consider themselves invincible. They simply do not realize the gruesome nature of the full-blown

And now we have had to face another pandemic. Unlike infection with HIV, everyone is at risk from COVID-19 because it is so easily transmissible. And also unlike AIDS, which was invariably fatal until a regimen of lifesaving drugs was developed, only a small percentage of those infected with COVID-19 have died. There is another, extremely important difference. AIDS personally affected only a small percentage of the American population, while COVID-19 disrupted all of our lives. But there are similarities as well. Once again there has been fear, sorrow, and anger. We were urged to protect ourselves and others, not with safe sex and condoms, but by social distancing and wearing masks. Once again, a public health disaster became a political issue. People were dying while our leaders played politics and jockeyed for position and personal advantage. AIDS took time. COVID-19 moved at warp speed. Instead of simply destroying lives, controversy about how to handle it seemed to destroy what

disease. How could they when they were not there? So there are still outbreaks of infections. In July 2012, the FDA approved a drug called Truvada for pre-exposure prophylaxis, or PrEP. Now there are other PrEP drugs as well. People who are HIV-negative but who feel they might become infected with HIV through sexual activity can take medication to reduce the risk of catching the virus to begin with. These days there are even advertisements on television for PrEP featuring attractive, relatable young people. And for those who do become infected, HAART therapy has become ever more effective with the development of new and better drugs since 1995. We have come a long way since the days of calling HIV the gay cancer.

ACT UP 30th anniversary march and rally, New York City, March 30, 2017.

remained of the bonds of civility and common cause that bound us together.

After months of denial and blatantly politicizing the COVID-19 pandemic, in mid-2020 the president of the United States finally did something right by authorizing the fast-track development of a vaccine to combat it. Forty years of HIV research provided the starting point. Building upon that knowledge, scientists were able to quickly refine and manufacture several different vaccines that effectively prevent COVID-19 hospitalizations for the vast majority of people. Without the prior AIDS research these vaccines could never have been developed so quickly. Since the vaccines were first made available in early 2021, Americans became increasingly divided between those who chose to protect themselves and their families and the people they encountered, and those who chose what they called their personal freedom over the common good. Now coronavirus has mutated into less lethal, but more contagious forms. As fear receded, people returned to normal activities, but the constantly mutating virus may become a permanent threat, like HIV. It is bitterly ironic that AIDS research made possible the COVID-19 vaccines but has not yet succeeded in producing a vaccine to prevent HIV infection. No one I knew during the AIDS horror would have refused *that* vaccine.

An entire generation of gay men was decimated by AIDS, and the survivors were forever changed. We came from every walk of life: businessmen, architects, teachers, doctors, bartenders, lawyers, plumbers, actors, contractors, musicians, salesmen, designers, factory workers, composers, deliverymen, artists, athletes, and more. There had always been outspoken homosexual individuals who lived their lives openly, and throughout the entire twentieth century there was a thriving underground gay subculture, particularly in the big cities. But before Gay Pride, the vast majority of gay people were invisible. They lived their daily lives in the closet because of homophobia. While there were activists before, it was an entire generation that came of age in the late 1960s and early '70s that

In many places in the rest of the world, the AIDS pandemic rages on.

- 26 million people were accessing antiretroviral therapy as of the end of June 2020.
- 37.7 million people were living with HIV in 2020.
- 1.5 million people became infected with HIV in 2020.
- 680,000 people died from AIDS-related illnesses in 2020.
- 76.2 million people have become infected with HIV since the start of the AIDS pandemic.
- A total of 33.5 million people have died from AIDS-related illnesses.

asserted and then openly lived the idea that gay people should be proud of who we are, and not ashamed of our natural orientation. We were the generation that refused to hide in the shadows and insisted upon equality. And over time, we have been fairly successful. A great majority of Americans now accept cisgender gay people without prejudice. After several decades of Gay Pride and increased visibility, most rational people began to understand that gay people are everywhere, and that almost certainly, someone they know and love is gay—a coworker, a social acquaintance, a friend, a relative, or sometimes even a parent. Familiarity and personal relationships have overcome bigotry for many people. But we were also the generation that tested the outer limits of sexual freedom, and because of a lethal microscopic virus we paid a terrible, bitter price.

The times are still changing. The cause of Gay Liberation scored a major success on June 26, 2015. In a blockbuster legal and cultural moment for the country, the Supreme Court ruled that same-sex couples in the United States, no matter where they live, have the same legal right to marry as different-sex couples. Today young children know what the word *gay* means. Celebrities proudly announce their sexuality. Questioning teens can find support. And now that we can legally marry and have children, it's almost shocking to remember that only a few decades ago, homosexual activities between consenting adults could get you arrested, and public exposure could ruin your life.

If only Americans could learn from the experience of the gay community and stop wasting time floundering in denial and wallowing in hatred. Throughout the AIDS crisis, the movement for equality and acceptance continued, but it was temporarily overshadowed by the challenge of coming to terms with the horrific carnage. Out of this struggle the AIDS generation of gay people made a community forged in pain and sorrow, tempered by compassion, and eventually resulting in a newfound strength and purpose. Today, as the crisis of the COVID-19 pandemic gradually recedes, the culture wars have ramped back up. The civil rights of lesbian, gay, bi, trans, and other queer people are once again under siege as our understanding of gender is evolving. In recent years there has been an explosion of people of all ages who identify as gender nonconforming, but this sea change has brought with it an enormous amount of confusion and resistance with hostile conservatives specifically targeting trans and nonbinary individuals. Opposition to same-sex marriage is still red meat for right-wing zealots, while the new reactionary Supreme Court majority seems poised to roll back the advances of the past few decades. Now young LGBTQ+ people who were born after the AIDS crisis are taking up the cause and are building upon the foundation we made to fight for a future with equality and respect for everyone.

HIV/AIDS IS NOW CONSIDERED TO BE ONE OF THE TOP FIVE DEADLIEST PANDEMICS IN ALL OF HUMAN HISTORY.

THERE STILL IS NO VACCINE. THERE STILL IS NO CURE.

The Origins of AIDS

In recent years scientists have pieced together the probable origins of HIV and how it became a pandemic. In the early twentieth century, somewhere in Central Africa, it is likely that a hunter killed a chimpanzee and butchered it for its meat. Perhaps the hunter cut himself, or the chimp scratched him, and somehow the chimp's blood got into the wound. The chimp was from a population infected with a retrovirus. The hunter became infected and later had sex and passed the virus on. From there it spread very slowly through the local human population by sexual contact. In retrospect we know from official records that by midcentury there were outbreaks of what we now call AIDS in Central Africa. Because there were no treatments, it was invariably fatal. It was called the "slim disease" because of the wasting syndrome.

Haiti has close ties with Africa. Like nearly all Black people in the Western Hemisphere, Haitians are descended from Africans who were trafficked and enslaved. But Haiti maintained close ties with Africa. At midcentury many Haitians lived in the former Belgian Congo. They had been recruited by the United Nations for work as civil servants because they spoke French, the official language of both countries. Some of them became infected with HIV through sexual contact with Africans. Some of those took the virus back to Haiti, where it spread slowly—all beneath the radar of medical science, because of an authoritarian regime and extreme poverty. And so, according to one theory, Haiti became the incubator for HIV in the Western Hemisphere.

Recent research has demonstrated that sometime around 1969, HIV began being passed back and forth between the United States and Haiti. Both Miami and New York have Haitian communities where the virus spread slowly, undetected, mainly between sex workers and their clients. In addition, during the 1970s, tainted medical blood products from Haiti were imported into the United States and contaminated part of the American blood supply. HIV entered the gay population when infected Haitians had sex with other men who were part of the hookup culture of easy, casual, recreational sex that had become a pervasive part of American urban gay life. And a thriving sex tourism industry brought infected gay Americans to Haiti, spreading the virus among sex workers there, raising issues of racism and economic exploitation.

Once the virus had taken hold in the American urban gay population, it spread rapidly as men passed the virus to their partners, and they passed it to theirs, and so on. Many affluent gay men were part of a circuit, traveling between New York, San Francisco, Los Angeles, and other cities for business or pleasure. During these trips they would also hook up for sex. And so, gradually, during the last half of the 1970s, the virus spread to the West Coast and other parts of the United States and Europe as well.

By the late 1970s, the unknown but lethal virus was now a pandemic on at least three continents. But in the United States it had found its ideal host population. HIV was spreading like wildfire among promiscuous, urban, gay men. It was a perfect storm. But because it took years to destroy their immune systems, no one even knew it existed until people started dying.

Author's Note

AIDS is the crucible living inside every gay writer old enough to remember it. It scratches away at our insides until we figure out how to wrestle with it. We must explain how we survived: mostly by dumb luck. And then do justice to the other half of our generation who did not—all those beautiful men who never made it past 40.

—Charles Kaiser, *New York Times*, February 7, 2021

The first summer of the COVID-19 pandemic was winding down. We were past the initial lockdowns and shocking waves of deaths, but vaccines were still in the future. Yolanda Scott, the publisher and editorial director of Charlesbridge Publishing, approached me with an idea—a book about the AIDS epidemic of the 1980s and 1990s for the COVID-19 generation of young people.

I am author/illustrator of fifteen nonfiction books for young readers. Ms. Scott was the editor of my last book, an illustrated YA biography of the great dancer and gay icon Vaslav Nijinsky. We had come to know one another quite well and enjoyed working together. She knew my history—that I lived through the AIDS years right in the epicenter of the plague, when AIDS was a certain death sentence. She was aware that I knew scores of people who suffered and died, among them nearly a dozen good friends and my own life partner. She suggested that of all established authors for young people, I was uniquely prepared to write about AIDS.

A project like the one she proposed would be a total departure from my previous work, and I had to think long and hard about whether or not I was willing to revisit that terrible time. Over a period of twenty-five years, many of the events of that era had faded in my memory. I had moved on and finally packed away the feelings of horror, grief, despair, and anger that all gay men of my generation lived with for so long.

I have a big extended family, and between them, my sister and brother have a total of nineteen grandchildren. My grandnieces and nephews are now either all grown up, or nearly so. I decided to attempt the project partly for them, young adults now living through the COVID-19 pandemic—so that they might understand how it was for me, growing up in a completely different world and living through a different pandemic.

I began by rereading Randy Shilts's magisterial account of the early years of the AIDS crisis, *And the Band Played On*. His book is a devastating indictment of the government's inaction in the face of appalling suffering and death. It rekindled my sorrow, anger, and disgust at the ignorance and hatred the gay community faced then and led to a realization that in many ways nothing has changed. Gay people are no longer vilified by a majority of Americans, but too many people still wallow in hatred, and the official responses to COVID-19 have demonstrated that ignorance, unfortunately, is eternal.

I am acutely aware that we—all of my friends and I—experienced the crisis of the AIDS years from a position of relative privilege. My partner, John, and I were both in our late thirties when our friends started dying. We both had successful careers and were reasonably comfortable financially. Most importantly, we had good health insurance and families who were supportive. Thousands of gay men did not have these advantages, and for them the AIDS years were even more terrible.

As I took a leap of faith and grappled with the idea of writing about AIDS, my approach gradually changed from an objective account of the epidemic to a completely subjective personal memoir.

I am a very reserved, even secretive person. But once committed, I was all in. When I unlocked the sealed box of memories and feelings, it all poured out in a great flood that I was at first unable and in the end unwilling to stop. So here it all is—the good, the bad, and the oh so ugly.

I would like to thank my oldest and best of friends, Doug Peix, who allowed me to tell his heart-wrenching story; Gail Dessimoz and Michael Racz, for their decades of friendship and moral support; Carol Bennett, Tim's daughter, who helped me recall the events in Laguna Beach; Mark Kane for his powerful words; my editor, Yolanda Scott, for proposing the idea and working with me to bring it to publication; and most particularly, my agent, Liz Nealon, who held my hand and encouraged me with invaluable support and sage advice as I was reliving the painful past and trying to put it all down in words.

I have embraced this project with a profound sense of humility and responsibility to the memory of my friends who were killed by this cruel disease, and I dedicate this book to them—all of the beautiful young men who touched my life, and who were robbed of the opportunity to grow old.

And in addition, I dedicate it to the memory of my dear longtime friends Tim Bennett and Richard Gillmore, who also lived through it all, and who have both died in recent years, long after the events in this book took place.

Musical References

"The Only Living Boy in New York"
Paul Simon, 1970

This beautiful song always resonated deeply with me during my early years in NYC when I was a relatively unsophisticated young man from the South making my way in the big city. I indulged the romantic notion of myself as the boy in the song. It still tugs at my heart.

"Disco Inferno"
The Trammps, 1976

This is one of the biggest disco hits from the mid-1970s, with a hard-driving beat and vocals that jump right out at you. It would typically be played fairly early in the evening to work up the crowd into a frenzy. It was included on the soundtrack of *Saturday Night Fever* in 1977— THE definitive disco movie starring John Travolta.

"California Dreamin'"
The Mamas & the Papas, 1965

My college years (1965–1969) coincided exactly with the rise of the counterculture. This was a huge megahit in the autumn of my freshman year, right at the moment when the youth of America were beginning to question the values of our society and rock and roll became the soundtrack of an entire generation. The Mamas & the Papas were the original celebrity hippies.

"Being Alive"
Stephen Sondheim, 1970

This is the showstopping song from Sondheim's Broadway musical *Company*, the story of a bachelor, Bobby, who is facing his thirty-fifth birthday and the prospect of living the rest of his life alone. He comes to the realization that "alone is alone, not alive," and decides that life is better lived with someone to love and be loved by. *Company* was one of the first Broadway shows I ever saw, and this song with its feeling of yearning and longing is a particular favorite of mine.

String Quartet No. 8 in E Minor, opus 59
Second movement, *Molto adagio*
Ludwig van Beethoven, 1808

This movement of the string quartet begins quietly with a hymn-like melody. As the music slowly unfolds, a rhythmic "heartbeat" emerges, and the individual strands become a somber, yet noble dirge. According to Carl Czerny, Beethoven's student, the theme of this movement occurred to the composer "as he contemplated the starry sky and thought of the Music of the Spheres." There is a profound sense of awe and wonder in this music that has always resonated deeply for me, and during the weeks when John Martin was dying, I listened to it over and over whenever I had a chance to be alone—and only when I was alone. This sublime piece of music became for me his elegy.

Source Notes

For more information about the sources below, see the bibliography on pages 151–154.

Page 1: Teen loses parents to COVID-19: Rodriguez, "Rest in Paradise," *USA Today*.

Page 2: US COVID-19 death statistics: Crist, "U.S. COVID-19 Deaths," WebMD, https://www.webmd.com/lung/news/20211122/us-covid-deaths-2021-surpass-2020-total.

Page 3: US HIV/AIDS statistics: "20 Years of AIDS," Center for Disease Control and Prevention (CDC), https://www.cdc.gov/media/pressrel/r010601.htm.

Page 11: History of the Stonewall National Monument: "Stonewall," National Park Service, https://www.nps.gov/ston/index.htm.

Page 14: Number of Americans killed and wounded in the Vietnam War: America's Wars Factsheet (Washington, D.C.: U.S. Department of Veterans Affairs, 2021), https://www.va.gov/opa/publications/factsheets/fs_americas_wars.pdf.

Page 42: Nick Rock is taken off life support: Shilts, p. 53.

Page 42: By the end of 1981, 270 cases and 121 deaths are reported due to mysterious illness: "A Timeline of HIV and AIDS," https://www.HIV.gov.

Page 48: In 1980, a huge new gay club called the Saint opens in New York: "The Saint," NYC LGBT Historic Sites Project.

Page 50: By the end of 1982, 772 cases and 618 deaths from AIDS are recorded in the US: "A Timeline of HIV and AIDS," https://www.HIV.gov.

Page 50: Growing concerns about HIV among health officials: Altman, "New Homosexual Disorder Worries Health Officials," *New York Times*.

Page 50: Hemophiliacs develop AIDS from donated blood: "Hemophilia," Mayo Clinic, https://www.mayoclinic.org/diseases -conditions/hemophilia/symptoms-causes/syc-20373327.

Page 51: In 1983, CDC reports on majority carriers and possible causes of AIDS: "A Timeline of HIV and AIDS," https://www.HIV.gov.

Page 53: Discovery of the retrovirus that causes AIDS: "A Timeline of HIV and AIDS," https://www. HIV.gov.

Page 53: In 1983, CDC reports on how HIV is transmitted: ibid.

Page 54: Progression of AIDS symptoms: "HIV/AIDS," Mayo Clinic, https://www.mayoclinic.org/diseases-conditions/hiv-aids/ symptoms-causes/syc-20373524.

Page 58: In 1983, a New York doctor is threatened with eviction for treating patients with AIDS, leading to the first AIDS discrimination lawsuit: ibid.

Page 59: In 1983, San Francisco General Hospital opens world's first dedicated AIDS ward: ibid.

Page 60: In 1982, Gay Men's Health Crisis (GMHC) organization is founded, https://www.GMHC.org.

Page 60: On October 8, 1983, 1,300 people attend a candlelit procession for AIDS victims in Washington, DC: United Press International, "Vigils Held for AIDS Victims," *New York Times*.

Page 62: In 1985, the blood test to detect HIV antibodies is approved by the FDA, leading to mixed individual and political reactions: Balzer, "The Times Poll: Tough New Government Action on AIDS Backed," *Los Angeles Times*.

Page 65: Annual pool party raises millions of dollars for AIDS research: Marin, "Beach Couple's Pool Party Always Makes a Splash of Cash for AIDS," *Los Angeles Times*.

Page 66: In 1985, Hemophiliac teenager Ryan White contracts AIDS and becomes nationwide face of AIDS education: "A Timeline of HIV and AIDS," https://www.HIV.gov.

Page 71: Press release announces celebrity Rock Hudson's terminal illness: Shilts, p. 575.

Page 72: Inaction of the Reagan administration: Shilts, p. 580.

Page 73: In 1985, Rock Hudson passes away: Shilts, chapter 57.

Page 73: Rock Hudson's death launches celebrity support for the American Foundation of AIDS Research: amfAR.

Page 76: In 1986, US government releases report on AIDS transmission and calls for education campaign: "A Timeline of HIV and AIDS," https://www.HIV.gov.

Page 78: In 1987, the NAMES Project is founded to create the AIDS Memorial Quilt: "The History of the Quilt," National AIDS Memorial, https://www.aidsmemorial.org/quilt-history.

Page 79: The AIDS Coalition to Unleash Power (ACT UP) is founded, coining the motto "Silence = Death": ACT UP, https://actupny.com.

Page 83: The first antiretroviral drug, AZT, is FDA approved to slow progress of HIV: Park, "The Story Behind the First AIDS Drug," *TIME*.

Page 83: President Reagan makes his first public policy speech about AIDS and establishes a Presidential Commission on HIV: "A Timeline of HIV and AIDS," https://www.HIV.gov.

Page 84: In 1987, the AIDS Memorial Quilt is displayed on the National Mall: "The History of the Quilt," National AIDS Memorial.

Page 92: By the early 1990s, several celebrities are infected with, or die from, AIDS: "A Timeline of HIV and AIDS": ibid.

Page 92: Government program provides care and services for low-income people with HIV: "Ryan White HIV/AIDS Program," Health Resources & Services Administration, https://ryan-white.hrsa.gov.

Page 92: In 1992, Sir Elton John establishes a nonprofit organization to fund prevention and treatment efforts: Elton John AIDS Foundation, https://www.eltonjohnaidsfoundation.org

Page 93: Rush Limbaugh and homophobia: Harris, "Let's Briefly Praise Rush Limbaugh—Then Bury Him Forever," *POLITICO*, https://www.politico.com/news/2021/02/17/rush-limbaugh-death-469726.

Page 116: In 1995, President Bill Clinton issues an executive order to establish a Presidential Advisory Council on HIV/AIDS: "A Timeline of HIV and AIDS," https://www.HIV.gov.

Page 116: A highly active antiviral therapy (HAART) is finally approved: "NCI Dictionary of Cancer Terms," National Cancer Institute, https://www.cancer.gov/publications/dictionaries/cancer-terms/expand/H.

Page 116: Within two years of HAART's approval, death rate plummets by nearly 50%: "A Timeline of HIV and AIDS," https://www.HIV.gov.

Page 117: By 1998, the AIDS-related mortality rate for African Americans is ten times that of white people, and three times that of Hispanic people: ibid.

Page 117: By the end of 2000, 774,467 people have been diagnosed with AIDS in the US and 448,060 have died: Center for Disease Control and Prevention (CDC). https://www.cdc.gov/media/pressrel/r010601.htm.

Page 117: In 1996, the AIDS Quilt is exhibited again in Washington, DC with 39,000 panels: "The History of the Quilt," National AIDS Memorial, https://www.aidsmemorial.org/quilt-history.

Page 133: In 2005, HIV immunity is found in 10% of people of European descent: "A Timeline of HIV and AIDS," https://www.HIV.gov.

Page 134: In 2012, the AIDS Quilt is exhibited again in Washington, DC with nearly 50,000 panels: ibid.

Page 135: In 2012, the FDA approves the drug Truvada for pre-exposure prophylaxis (PrEP) to prevent HIV transmission: ibid.

Page 136: HIV research and COVID-19 vaccines: Zuckerman and McKay, "How HIV Research Laid the Foundation for Covid Vaccines," *Wall Street Journal*.

Page 137: Global HIV and AIDS statistics: "Fact Sheet," UNAIDS.

Page 139: HIV/AIDS is one of the top five deadliest pandemics in human history: "History's Worst Global Pandemics," Public Health Online, https://www.publichealthonline.org/worst-globalpandemics-in-history/.

Page 140: Possible Central African origin of HIV: Shilts, p. 510.

Page 140: Haiti as incubator for HIV: Shilts, p. 393.

Page 141: Spread of HIV in the 1970s: McNeill, "HIV Arrived in the U.S. Long Before Patient Zero," *New York Times*.

Page 146: "as he contemplated . . . the Music of the Spheres": Thayer, *The Life of Ludwig van Beethoven*, pp. 74-75.

Select Bibliography

Books

Bianchi, Tom. *Tom Bianchi: Fire Island Pines: Polaroids 1975–1983*. Bologna: Damiani, 2013.

Shilts, Randy. *And the Band Played On: Politics, People, and the AIDS Epidemic*. New York: St. Martin's Griffin, 2007.

Wheelock Thayer, Alexander. *The Life of Ludwig van Beethoven*, vol. 2. Translated by Henry Edward Krehbiel. New York: The Beethoven Association, 1934. https://www.gutenberg.org/files/43592/43592-h/43592-h.htm.

Newspaper Articles

Altman, Lawrence. "New Homosexual Disorder Worries Health Officials." *New York Times*, May 11, 1982.

Altman, Lawrence. "Rare Cancer Seen in 41 Homosexuals." *New York Times*, July 3, 1981.

Balzer, John. "The Times Poll: Tough New Government Action on AIDS Backed." *Los Angeles Times*, Dec. 19, 1985.

Hirsley, Michael. "Talk of AIDS Quarantine Spreads Like a Disease." *Chicago Tribune*, Nov. 12, 1985.

Mandeville, Aproova. "HIV Death Rates Fell by Half, CDC Says." *New York Times*, Nov. 19, 2020.

Marin, Pamela. "Beach Couple's Pool Party Always Makes a Splash of Cash for AIDS." *Los Angeles Times*, Sept. 13, 1991.

McNeill, Donald G. Jr. "HIV Arrived in the U.S. Long Before Patient Zero." *New York Times*, Oct. 26, 2016.

Nagourney, Adam. "Was Reagan a Precursor to Trump? A New Documentary Says Yes." *New York Times*, Nov. 11, 2020.

Quammen, David. "The Pandemic from the Virus's Point of View." *New York Times*, Sept. 21, 2020.

United Press International. "Vigils Held for AIDS Victims." *New York Times*, Oct. 9, 1983.

Zuckerman, Gregory and Betsy McKay. "How HIV Research Laid the Foundation for Covid Vaccines." *Wall Street Journal*, Dec. 24, 2020.

Online Articles

Crist, Carolyn. "U.S. COVID-19 Deaths in 2021 Surpass 2020 Total." *WebMD*, Nov. 22, 2021. https://www.webmd.com/lung/news/20211122/us-covid-deaths-2021-surpass-2020-total.

Harris, John F. "Let's Briefly Praise Rush Limbaugh—Then Bury Him Forever." *POLITICO*, Feb. 17, 2021. https://www.politico.com/news/2021/02/17/rush-limbaugh-death-469726.

Henrikson, Maggi. "The House with a Colorful History." *Stu News Laguna*, Nov. 27, 2020. https://www.stunewslaguna.com/6322-the-house-with-a-colorful-history-081018.

Park, Alice. "The Story Behind the First AIDS Drug." *Time.* Mar. 19, 2017. https://time.com/4705809/first-aids-drug-azt.

Rodriguez, Adrianna. "'Rest in Paradise': Georgia Teen Loses His Mom and Dad to COVID-19 in Same Week." *USA Today*, Aug. 3, 2020. https://www.usatoday.com/story/news/nation/2020/08/03/covid-georgia-teen-loses-both-parents-coronavirus-same-week/5571493002.

Websites

"20 Years of AIDS: 450,000 Americans Dead, Over 1 Million Have Been Infected." *Center for Disease Control and Prevention*. Last reviewed June 1, 2001. https://www.cdc.gov/media/pressrel/r010601.htm.

America's Wars Factsheet. Washington, D.C.: U.S. Department of Veterans Affairs, 2021. https://www.va.gov/opa/publications/factsheets/fs_americas_wars.pdf.

"HAART." *National Cancer Institute.* Accessed June 16, 2022. https://www.cancer.gov/publications/dictionaries/cancer-terms/expand/H.

"Hemophilia." *Mayo Clinic.* Posted Oct. 7, 2021. https://www.mayoclinic.org/diseases-conditions/hemophilia/symptoms-causes/syc-20373327.

"History." *Gay Men's Health Crisis.* Accessed June 16, 2022. https://www.gmhc.org/history.

"The History of the Quilt." *National AIDS Memorial*. Accessed Apr. 27, 2022. https://www.aidsmemorial.org/quilt-history.

"History's Worst Global Pandemics." *Public Health Online.* Accessed July 13, 2022. https://www.publichealthonline.org/worst-global-pandemics-in-history/.

"HIV/AIDS." *Mayo Clinic.* Last reviewed July 29, 2022. https://www.mayoclinic.org/diseases-conditions/hiv-aids/symptoms-causes/syc-20373524.

Origin of HIV and AIDS. Last updated Aug. 25, 2022. https://www.beintheknow.org/.

"Ryan White HIV/AIDS Program." *Health Resources and Services Administration.* Accessed Apr. 27, 2022. https://ryanwhite.hrsa.gov.

"Stonewall National Monument." *National Park Service.* Last updated Apr. 17, 2022. https://www.nps.gov/ston/index.htm.

"A Timeline of HIV and AIDS." *HIV.gov.* Accessed Apr. 27, 2022. https://www.hiv.gov/hiv-basics/overview/history/hiv-and-aids-timeline.

General Websites

actupny.com

amfar.org

www.eltonjohnaidsfoundation.org

www.nyclgbtsites.org

www.publichealthonline.org

www.unaids.org

www.webmd.com

Image Credits

Jacket: (top middle) Carol Bennett, (2nd row, left) National Institutes of Health, (3rd row, middle) John Green.

pp. 13, 67: Associated Press.

pp. 17, 120, 122: Doug Peix.

pp. 32–33: Bill Bernstein.

pp. 54–55: San Francisco Chronicle/Hearst Newspapers via Getty Images.

pp. 56–57: Fairfax Media Archives/Getty Images.

p. 61: John Green.

p. 70: ScreenProd/Photononstop/Alamy Stock Photo.

p. 72: Chris Hunter/Associated Press.

pp. 74–75: Carol Bennett.

p. 79: Chester Higgins Jr./New York Times/Redux.

p. 80: Charlie J Ercilla/Alamy Stock Photo.

p. 82: Martin Keene/PA Images/Alamy Stock Photo.

p. 104: National Institutes of Health.

p. 115: Nicholas Atkins.

pp. 118, 131, 132 (paintings): Lynn Curlee.

p. 136: SIPA/Associated Press.

All remaining photos courtesy of Lynn Curlee.

Index